Clover
Series

FIRST TRY
FOR THE TOEIC®
L&R TEST

Robert Hickling

JN126084

KINSEIDO

Kinseido Publishing Co., Ltd.

3-21 Kanda Jimbo-cho, Chiyoda-ku,
Tokyo 101-0051, Japan

First published 2023 by Kinseido Publishing Co., Ltd.

Design   Nampoosha Co., Ltd.

音声ファイル無料ダウンロード

https://www.kinsei-do.co.jp/download/4182

この教科書で DL 00 の表示がある箇所の音声は、上記 URL または QR コードにて
無料でダウンロードできます。自習用音声としてご活用ください。

▶ PC からのダウンロードをお勧めします。スマートフォンなどでダウンロードされる場合は、
　ダウンロード前に「解凍アプリ」をインストールしてください。
▶ URL は 検索ボックスではなくアドレスバー (URL 表示欄) に入力してください。
▶ お使いのネットワーク環境によってはダウンロードできない場合があります。

CD 00　左記の表示がある箇所の音声は、教室用 CD (Class Audio CD) に収録されています。

はじめに

FIRST TRY FOR THE TOEIC® L&R TEST は、*TOEIC®* Listening and Reading Test (以下、TOEIC L&Rテスト) でスコア350以上を目指す学習者のみなさんにふさわしい内容になっています。本のタイトルが示すように、はじめてテストを受験しようとしていて、テストの形式や問題のタイプに慣れていない人には特に役に立ちます。また、リスニングやリーディングの基礎力を伸ばしたいという人にも適しています。

この本は15章で構成されており、テストと同様に各章はリスニングセクション (Part 1-4) とリーディングセクション (Part 5-7) に分かれています (TOEIC L&Rテストについてはp.10-11をご覧ください)。トピックは「ショッピング」「旅行」「会議・打ち合わせ」など、実際のテストでよく登場するものを中心に扱っています。

語彙はTOEICに欠かせない要素です。そこで、この本ではトピックに関連したやさしいレベルの重要語句を、リスニングセクションとリーディングセクションの冒頭で取り上げています。また、文法ももうひとつの重要な要素です。そのため、各章のPart 5に文法説明のセクションを特別に設けてあります。

すべてのパートにはウォームアップ用の簡単なアクティビティ (Warming Up) が用意されており、リスニングセクションでは聴解のためのディクテーション、リーディングセクションでは読解のためのさまざまな選択式の問題に取り組みます。その上で、実戦形式の問題 (Now You Try!) に挑戦します。

本書は対象レベルの学習者を念頭に置いて書かれているため、複雑な文や長い文、難しい語彙は基本的に登場しません。また、文法も徐々に難しくなるよう全体的に配慮してあります。Part 5以外の各パートには、問題を解くのに役立つヒントも書かれています。

本書が学習者のみなさんの英語力向上とTOEIC L&Rテストの準備に役立つことを心から願っています。

ロバート・ヒックリング

本書は CheckLink（チェックリンク）対応テキストです。

CheckLinkのアイコンが表示されている設問は、CheckLinkに対応しています。
CheckLinkを使用しなくても従来通りの授業ができますが、特色をご理解いただき、授業活性化のためにぜひご活用ください。

CheckLinkの特色について

　大掛かりで複雑な従来のe-learningシステムとは異なり、CheckLinkのシステムは大きな特色として次の3点が挙げられます。
1. これまで行われてきた教科書を使った授業展開に大幅な変化を加えることなく、専門的な知識なしにデジタル学習環境を導入することができる。
2. PC教室やCALL教室といった最新の機器が導入された教室に限定されることなく、普通教室を使用した授業でもデジタル学習環境を導入することができる。
3. 授業中での使用に特化し、教師・学習者双方のモチベーション・集中力をアップさせ、授業自体を活性化することができる。

▶教科書を使用した授業に「デジタル学習環境」を導入できる

　本システムでは、学習者は教科書のCheckLinkのアイコンが表示されている設問にPCやスマートフォン、アプリからインターネットを通して解答します。そして教師は、授業中にリアルタイムで解答結果を把握し、正解率などに応じて有効な解説を行うことができるようになっています。教科書自体は従来と何ら変わりはありません。解答の手段としてCheckLinkを使用しない場合でも、従来通りの教科書として使用して授業を行うことも、もちろん可能です。

▶教室環境を選ばない

　従来の多機能なe-learning教材のように学習者側の画面に多くの機能を持たせることはせず、「解答する」ことに機能を特化しました。PCだけでなく、一部タブレット端末やスマートフォン、アプリからの解答も可能です。したがって、PC教室やCALL教室といった大掛かりな教室は必要としません。普通教室でもCheckLinkを用いた授業が可能です。教師はPCだけでなく、一部タブレット端末やスマートフォンからも解答結果の確認をすることができます。

▶授業を活性化するための支援システム

　本システムは予習や復習のツールとしてではなく、授業中に活用されることで真価を発揮する仕組みになっています。CheckLinkというデジタル学習環境を通じ、教師と学習者双方が授業中に解答状況などの様々な情報を共有することで、学習者はやる気を持って解答し、教師は解答状況に応じて効果的な解説を行う、という好循環を生み出します。CheckLinkは、普段の授業をより活力のあるものへと変えていきます。

　上記3つの大きな特色以外にも、掲示板などの授業中に活用できる機能を用意しています。従来通りの教科書としても使用はできますが、ぜひCheckLinkの機能をご理解いただき、普段の授業をより活性化されたものにしていくためにご活用ください。

CheckLink の使い方

CheckLink は、PC や一部のタブレット端末、スマートフォン、アプリを用いて、この教科書にある
⟲CheckLink のアイコン表示のある設問に解答するシステムです。
・初めて CheckLink を使う場合、以下の要領で**「学習者登録」**と**「教科書登録」**を行います。
・一度登録を済ませれば、あとは毎回**「ログイン画面」**から入るだけです。CheckLink を使う
　教科書が増えたときだけ、改めて**「教科書登録」**を行ってください。

CheckLink URL

https://checklink.kinsei-do.co.jp/student/

登録は CheckLink 学習者用
アプリが便利です。ダウン
ロードはこちらから ▶▶▶

▶学習者登録 （PC ／タブレット／スマートフォンの場合)

①上記 URL にアクセスすると、右のページが表示されます。学校名を入力し
　「ログイン画面へ」を選択してください。
　PC の場合は「PC 用はこちら」を選択して PC 用ページを表示します。同
　様に学校名を入力し「ログイン画面へ」を選択してください。
②ログイン画面が表示されたら「**初めての方はこちら」**を選択し
　「学習者登録画面」に入ります。

③自分の学籍番号、氏名、メールアドレス（学校
　のメールなど**PC メールを推奨**)を入力し、次
　に**任意のパスワード**を 8 桁以上 20 桁未満（半
　角英数字）で入力します。なお、学籍番号は
　パスワードとして使用することはできません。
④「パスワード確認」は、❸で入力したパスワー
　ドと同じものを入力します。
⑤最後に「登録」ボタンを選択して登録は完了
　です。次回からは、「ログイン画面」から学籍
　番号とパスワードを入力してログインしてく
　ださい。

▶教科書登録

①ログイン後、メニュー画面から「教科書登録」を選び（PCの場合はその後「新規登録」ボタンを選択）、「教科書登録」画面を開きます。

②教科書と受講する授業を登録します。
教科書の最終ページにある、**教科書固有番号**のシールをはがし、印字された**16桁の数字とアルファベット**を入力します。

③授業を担当される先生から連絡された**11桁の授業ID**を入力します。

④最後に「登録」ボタンを選択して登録は完了です。

⑤実際に使用する際は「教科書一覧」（PCの場合は「教科書選択画面」）の該当する教科書名を選択すると、「問題解答」の画面が表示されます。

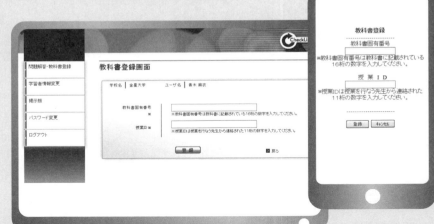

▶問題解答

①問題は教科書を見ながら解答します。この教科書の ⟲CheckLink のアイコン表示のある設問に解答できます。

②問題が表示されたら選択肢を選びます。

③表示されている問題に解答した後、「解答」ボタンを選択すると解答が登録されます。

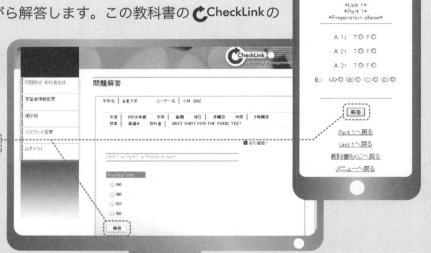

▶CheckLink 推奨環境

PC

推奨 OS
　Windows 7, 10 以降
　MacOS X 以降

推奨ブラウザ
　Internet Explorer 8.0 以上
　Firefox 40.0 以上
　Google Chrome 50 以上
　Safari

携帯電話・スマートフォン
　3G 以降の携帯電話（docomo, au, softbank）
　iPhone, iPad（iOS9 〜）
　Android OS スマートフォン、タブレット

・最新の推奨環境についてはウェブサイトをご確認ください。
・上記の推奨環境を満たしている場合でも、機種によってはご利用いただけない場合もあります。また、
　推奨環境は技術動向等により変更される場合があります。

▶CheckLink 開発

CheckLink は奥田裕司 福岡大学教授、正興 IT ソリューション株式会社、株式会社金星堂に
よって共同開発されました。

CheckLink は株式会社金星堂の登録商標です。

CheckLink の使い方に関するお問い合わせは…

正興 IT ソリューション株式会社　CheckLink 係

e-mail　checklink@seiko-denki.co.jp

FIRST TRY FOR THE TOEIC® L&R TEST

Contents

TOEIC® Listening and Reading テストについて

- TOEICとは、Test of English for International Communicationの略称で、「英語によるコミュニケーション能力」を総合的に評価するテストです。
- 実際のテストでは、リスニング100問（約45分間）、リーディング100問（75分間）の計200問を約2時間で解きます（休憩はありません）。
- マークシート方式で、問題はすべて英語で構成されています。
- 出題内容は、日常的な話題からビジネスのシチュエーションまで多岐にわたりますが、特殊なビジネスの知識を必要とする問題は出題されません。
- スコアは10～990まで5ポイント刻みで算出されます。

◆ 問題形式について

リスニングセクション（約45分間：100問）＊	
Part 1	**写真描写問題：6問** • 1枚の写真について4つの短い英文を聞いて、最も適切に描写しているものを選びます。 • 英文は印刷されていません。
Part 2	**応答問題：25問** • 1つの質問（または発言）と3つの応答を聞いて、最も適切な応答を選びます。 • 質問および応答は印刷されていません。
Part 3	**会話問題：39問**（1つの会話につき3つの設問×13セット） • 2人または3人の人物による会話と設問を聞いて、選択肢から最も適切な答えを選びます。 • 会話中の表現の意図を問う問題が出題されます（意図問題）。 • 注文書、グラフ、地図など図表を見て答える問題が出題されます（図表問題）。 • 会話は印刷されていません（設問および選択肢は印刷されています）。
Part 4	**説明文問題：30問**（1つの説明文につき3つの設問×10セット） • アナウンスやナレーションなどのトークと設問を聞いて、選択肢から最も適切な答えを選びます。 • トーク中の表現の意図を問う問題が出題されます（意図問題）。 • 注文書、グラフ、地図など図表を見て答える問題が出題されます（図表問題）。 • トークは印刷されていません（設問および選択肢は印刷されています）。

＊音声はアメリカ、イギリス、カナダ、オーストラリアの発音です。

	リーディングセクション（75分間：100問）
Part 5	**短文穴埋め問題：30問** • 短い文の中に空所が1つあります。 • 空所に入る最も適切な選択肢を選んで文を完成させます。
Part 6	**長文穴埋め問題：16問** • 長文の中に空所が4つあります。 • 空所に入る最も適切な選択肢を選んで文を完成させます。 • 文書中に入る適切な語句または文を選択する問題が出題されます（文選択問題）。
Part 7	**読解問題：54問**（1つの文書：29問、複数の文書：25問） • Eメールや広告、記事などのさまざまな文書と設問を読み、選択肢から最も適切な答えを選びます。 • 1つの文書（シングルパッセージ）を読んで答えるものと、2〜3つの関連する文書（ダブルパッセージ／トリプルパッセージ）を読んで答えるものの2タイプがあります。 • チャット形式など、複数の人物によるやりとりに関する問題が出題されます。 • 文書中の表現の意図を問う問題が出題されます（意図問題）。 • 文を挿入する適切な位置を選択する問題が出題されます（文挿入問題）。 • 1つの文書では2〜4問、複数の文書では5問の設問があります。

なお、一般受験の *TOEIC*® Listening and Reading 公開テストのほかに、企業や学校向けの団体特別受験「IPテスト」があります。IPテストでは過去に公開テストで出題された問題を使用します。

Shopping

トピック 買い物 文法 名詞

Vocabulary Builder A

CheckLink DL 002 CD1-02

次の 1 ～ 8 の意味に合うものを a ～ h から選びましょう。その後で、音声を聞いて答えを確認しましょう。

1. discount (　　)　　**2.** customer (　　)　　**3.** item (　　)　　**4.** on sale (　　)

5. receipt (　　)　　**6.** order (　　)　　**7.** shopper (　　)　　**8.** selection (　　)

a. 買い物客	**b.** セール中で	**c.** 選択、選ばれたもの	**d.** 客
e. 品物、商品	**f.** 注文（する）	**g.** 領収書、レシート	**h.** 割引（く）

Part 1 Photographs 【写真描写問題】

Part 1 で出題される文の多くは、"He **is working**." や "The children **are playing**." のように現在進行形で人物の動作を表します。ここでは 1 人の人物の動作を考えてみましょう。

Warming Up

CheckLink DL 003 CD1-03

音声を聞いて空所の語句を書き取り、写真を最も適切に描写しているものを選びましょう。

(A) The man is _____ a banana.

(B) The man is _____ a shopping list.

(C) The man is _____ food.

(D) The man is _____ some fruit.

Now You Try!

CheckLink DL 004 ～ 005 CD1-04 ～ CD1-05

写真を描写する 4 つの音声を聞いて、最も適切なものを選びましょう。

❶

Ⓐ Ⓑ Ⓒ Ⓓ

❷

Ⓐ Ⓑ Ⓒ Ⓓ

Part 2 Question-Response 【応答問題】

be動詞（am、is、are、was、were）やdo、does、didで始まる疑問文は、たいていYesかNo
で答えることができます。答えとなる内容はYesなのかNoなのか、よく聞きましょう。

Warming Up CheckLink DL 006 ~ 007 CD1-06 ~ CD1-07

音声を聞いて空所の語句を書き取り、質問に対する最も適切な応答を選びましょう。

1. Are these shirts on sale?

　(A) No, _____ T-shirts.

　(B) Yes, _____ is on sale.

　(C) Yes, a _____ .

2. Do you sell pet food?

　(A) Yes, we _____ .

　(B) No, dogs and _____ .

　(C) Yes, we sell _____ .

Now You Try! CheckLink DL 008 ~ 011 CD1-08 ~ CD1-11

質問とそれに対する3つの応答を聞いて、最も適切なものを選びましょう。

1. Ⓐ Ⓑ Ⓒ　　**2.** Ⓐ Ⓑ Ⓒ　　**3.** Ⓐ Ⓑ Ⓒ　　**4.** Ⓐ Ⓑ Ⓒ

Part 3 Conversations 【会話問題】

Part 3 の会話の冒頭の文はいつも特に注意して聞きましょう。たいていの場合、最初の文で
どんな場面かわかるので、会話についていきやすくなります。

Warming Up CheckLink DL 012 ~ 013 CD1-12 ~ CD1-13

音声を聞いて空所の語句を書き取り、質問に対する最も適切な答えを選びましょう。

> **M:** I'm going to the convenience ^{1}_____ for some milk. Do you need
> ^{2}_____?
>
> **W:** Could you get some ^{3}_____ and a carton of ^{4}_____?
>
> **M:** Sure. I'll be back in half an ^{5}_____ .

1. Where will the man go?

　(A) To a bakery　　(B) To a supermarket

　(C) To a convenience store　　(D) To a department store

2. What does the woman want?

　(A) Milk　　(B) Milk and bread

　(C) Bread and eggs　　(D) Milk and eggs

3. When will the man return home?

　(A) In 10 minutes　(B) In 30 minutes　(C) In 60 minutes　(D) In 90 minutes

Now You Try!

CheckLink   DL 014 ~ 017   CD1-14 ~ CD1-17

会話を聞いて、質問に対する最も適切な答えを選びましょう。

Conversation 1

1. What are the speakers talking about?

(A) A sweater

(B) A shirt

(C) A dress

(D) A skirt

2. What does the man like?

(A) The size

(B) The color

(C) The price

(D) The design

3. What will the man do next?

(A) Try on the item

(B) Look for a different color

(C) Buy the item

(D) Leave the store

Conversation 2

4. Where is the man?

(A) At a department store

(B) At a computer store

(C) At a flower shop

(D) At a bank

5. Why does the man return the item?

(A) He does not like coffee.

(B) It is broken.

(C) He does not like the color.

(D) It is the wrong size.

6. What does the woman ask the man for?

(A) His name

(B) His member's card

(C) His receipt

(D) His credit card

Part 4 Talks

【説明文問題】

トークが流れる前に、telephone message や advertisement など、これから聞くトークの種類が述べられます。気持ちの準備ができるので、どのような種類があるかできるだけたくさん覚えましょう。

例：announcement（お知らせ）/ broadcast（放送）/ news report（ニュース報道）/
excerpt from a meeting（会議の抜粋）

Warming Up

CheckLink   DL 018 ~ 019   CD1-18 ~ CD1-19

音声を聞いて空所の語句を書き取り、質問に対する最も適切な答えを選びましょう。

Attention ¹_____. The store will be ²_____ in fifteen ³_____.
Please bring your final ⁴_____ to the cashier now. Thank you for
⁵_____ at RightFit Fashions. We look forward to ⁶_____ you again soon.

NOTE cashier レジ係

1. Who is the speaker?
(A) A customer
(B) A waiter
(C) A teacher
(D) A store manager

2. What will happen in 15 minutes?
(A) A sale will start.
(B) A sale will end.
(C) The store will open.
(D) The store will close.

3. What will listeners probably do?
(A) Bring a receipt
(B) Buy a fashion magazine
(C) Ask for a discount
(D) Go to the cashier

Now You Try!

  CheckLink DL 020 ~ 023 CD1-20 ~ CD1-23

説明文を聞いて、質問に対する最も適切な答えを選びましょう。

Talk 1

1. What is the speaker announcing?
(A) A grand opening sale
(B) A winter sale
(C) A spring sale
(D) A closing sale

2. What can listeners get?
(A) A discount
(B) Free drinks
(C) A price list
(D) Free items

3. When does the sale end?
(A) On Thursday
(B) On Friday
(C) On Saturday
(D) On Sunday

Talk 2

4. Where does the speaker work?
(A) At a jewelry store
(B) At a bookshop
(C) At a garden shop
(D) At a furniture store

5. What does the speaker tell the listener?
(A) A book is in the store.
(B) He needs her address.
(C) He will call again.
(D) He made a mistake.

6. What will the listener bring?
(A) Her receipt
(B) Her library card
(C) Her book
(D) Her order number

Vocabulary Builder (B)

CheckLink   DL 024   CD1-24

次の 1 ～ 8 の意味に合うものを a ～ h から選びましょう。その後で、音声を聞いて答えを確認しましょう。

1. coupon（　） **2.** shop（　） **3.** save（　） **4.** feedback（　）
5. equipment（　） **6.** product（　） **7.** payment（　） **8.** tool（　）

a. 支払い	**b.** 製品	**c.** 道具	**d.** 店、買い物をする
e. 節約する	**f.** 割引券	**g.** 意見、反応	**h.** 機器、用品

Part 5 Sentence Completion 【短文穴埋め問題】

名詞は文の中で主語や目的語として使うことができます。また、名詞には数えられるものと数えられないものがあります。

名詞が主語になる場合

● 主語とは動作を行う人や物のことです。
*A **car** runs.*（名詞 car は動作を行う）
● 主語の後ろに be 動詞が続く場合は状態を表します。
*The **car** is new.*（名詞 car の状態を表す）

名詞が目的語になる場合

● 目的語とは動作を受ける人や物のことです。
*I drive a **car**.*（名詞 car は動作を受ける）

数えられる名詞

● ほとんどの名詞には単数形と複数形があります。
book-books   watch-watches   potato-potatoes   country-countries   child-children
● 単数形と一緒に使える語句 ➡ **a/an, the, one**
a peach   an apple   the class   one student
● 複数形と一緒に使える語句 ➡ **the, two/three …, some, several, a lot of, many, a few**
two boys   some apples   several chairs   a lot of tests   many students   a few cities

数えられない名詞

● 数えられない名詞は形が変わりません。
bread   homework   information   jewelry   love   money   snow   water   weather
● 数えられない名詞と一緒に使える語句 ➡ **the, some, a lot of, much, little**
the weather   some water   a lot of snow   much money   little information

名詞の見分け方

● 以下のように、単語の終わりの形で名詞を見分けることができる場合もあります。
train**er**   doct**or**   scient**ist**   move**ment**   happi**ness**   educa**tion**   vi**sion**
experi**ence**   assist**ance**   nationa**lity**

Warming Up

CheckLink

日本語の意味に合うように、正しい選択肢を選びましょう。

1. 数人の作業員：a few (**a.** worker   **b.** workers)

2. たくさんの楽しみ：a lot of (**a.** enjoy   **b.** enjoyment)

3. 1つの活動：an (**a.** active   **b.** activity)

4. 大きな違い：a big (**a.** difference   **b.** different)

5. 素晴らしい決断：an excellent (**a.** decide   **b.** decision)

Now You Try!

CheckLink

4つの選択肢から最も適切な選択肢を選び、文を完成させましょう。

1. The ------- is very popular in this pet shop.
   (A) produces   (B) produced   (C) producing   (D) product

2. A new ------- opened in the Green Forest mall.
   (A) shopper   (B) shop   (C) shopping   (D) shopped

3. A ------- buys vegetables here every day.
   (A) customer   (B) customize   (C) customizing   (D) customized

4. People make many cashless ------- now.
   (A) pay   (B) paying   (C) payments   (D) payer

5. The department store has a ------- in January.
   (A) sale   (B) sell   (C) sales   (D) selling

6. There are many fashionable shops in the -------.
   (A) build   (B) building   (C) built   (D) builder

7. The store has an excellent ------- of toys.
   (A) select   (B) selecting   (C) selected   (D) selection

8. Some ------- about the new shopping center is on the Web site.
   (A) inform   (B) informing   (C) information   (D) informed

Part **6**   Text Completion 　　　　　　　　　　【長文穴埋め問題】

Part 6 では、空所のある文だけを読んで意味を考えることで正しい選択肢を選べる場合があります。

 **Warming Up** 　　　　　　　　　　　　　　　　　　　　 ⟲CheckLink

正しい選択肢を選び、文を完成させましょう。

1. Most of the store's (**a.** prices   **b.** products) are on sale.

2. First Sports (**a.** plays   **b.** sells) tennis equipment.

3. Value Footwear has a great (**a.** selection   **b.** size) of women's shoes.

4. This shopping center is always (**a.** busy   **b.** new) on weekends.

Now You Try! 　　　　　　　　　　　　　　　　　　　　 ⟲CheckLink

4 つの選択肢から最も適切な選択肢を選び、文を完成させましょう。

Questions 1–4 refer to the following article.

Online shopping is very ------- now. You do not need any special computer -------,
　　　　　　　　　　　　　　1.　　　　　　　　　　　　　　　　　　　**2.**

and shopping is quick and easy. For some people, online shopping can be -------.
　　　　　　　　　　　　　　　　　　　　　　　　　　　　　　　　　　　　　3.

Luckily, however, you can shop safely. -------.
　　　　　　　　　　　　　　　　4.

---

1. (A) heavy　　　　(B) bright　　　　(C) early　　　　(D) common

2. (A) skills　　　　(B) games　　　　(C) problems　　　　(D) cases

3. (A) large　　　　(B) pretty　　　　(C) dangerous　　　　(D) modern

4. (A) It is a nice shop.

　　 (B) Visit our Web site for great advice.

　　 (C) Tell us your name and address.

　　 (D) You will not save money.

Part 7 Reading Comprehension 【読解問題】

Part 6やPart 7では、文書の前にe-mail、letter、memoなど文書のタイプが書いてあります。
それぞれの意味を覚えておくと、どのような内容の文を読むのか前もって準備できます。

Warming Up
CheckLink

次の 1 ～ 8 の意味に合うものを a ～ h から選びましょう。

1. advertisement（　）　**2.** article（　）　**3.** brochure（　）　**4.** instructions（　）
5. form（　）　**6.** notice（　）　**7.** review（　）　**8.** text-message chain（　）

a. 記事　　　**b.** レビュー　　　**c.** お知らせ、通知　　　**d.** パンフレット
e. 指示書　　**f.** 広告　　　**g.** テキストメッセージのやりとり　　**h.** 用紙

Now You Try!
CheckLink

文書を読んで、設問に対する最も適切な答えを選びましょう。

Questions 1–2 refer to the following e-mail.

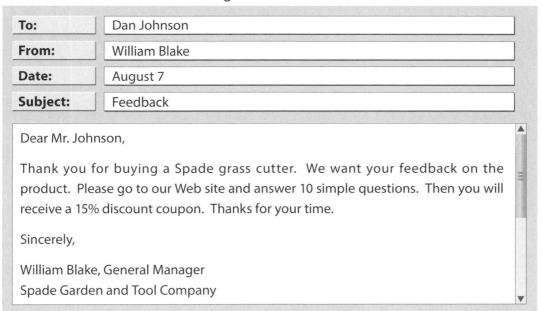

To:	Dan Johnson
From:	William Blake
Date:	August 7
Subject:	Feedback

Dear Mr. Johnson,

Thank you for buying a Spade grass cutter. We want your feedback on the product. Please go to our Web site and answer 10 simple questions. Then you will receive a 15% discount coupon. Thanks for your time.

Sincerely,

William Blake, General Manager
Spade Garden and Tool Company

1. What did Mr. Johnson buy?

(A) A gardening tool　(B) A flower box　(C) An outdoor table　(D) Some plants

2. What will Mr. Johnson do for a discount coupon?

(A) Show a receipt　(B) Use a card　(C) Buy some flowers　(D) Answer questions

Questions 3–4 refer to the following letter.

Style 1 Clothing Company

6215 Dunbar Street
Toronto, Ontario
M5A OM9

July 4

Dear Ms. Mills,

Thank you for becoming a Style 1 Points Program member. You get points for shopping at our store. You also receive double points on the 10th day of every month. Please come again soon!

Best regards,

Catherine Walker
Sales Manager, Style 1 Clothing Company

3. What is the letter about?

(A) A sale   (B) A points program   (C) A new store   (D) Summer clothes

4. When can Ms. Mills receive double points?

(A) June 1   (B) July 4   (C) August 10   (D) September 30

Dining Out

 トピック 食事 〉 文法 代名詞

Vocabulary Builder Ⓐ

🔄 CheckLink 🎧 DL 025 💿 CD1-25

次の1〜8の意味に合うものをa〜hから選びましょう。その後で、音声を聞いて答えを確認しましょう。

1. prepare （　）　　**2.** serve （　）　　**3.** meal （　）　　**4.** crowded （　）

5. reservation （　）　　**6.** confirm （　）　　**7.** suggest （　）　　**8.** ready （　）

a. 食事	**b.** 予約	**c.** 提案する	**d.** 料理を出す
e. 混雑している	**f.** 準備する	**g.** 準備ができた	**h.** 確認する

Part 1 Photographs 【写真描写問題】

2人の人物が写っている写真の場合、"They're …" "The men are …" "The women are …" などと聞こえたら、2人に共通している動作に注目しましょう。

 ### Warming Up

🔄 CheckLink 🎧 DL 026 💿 CD1-26

音声を聞いて空所の語句を書き取り、写真を最も適切に描写しているものを選びましょう。

(A) They're _____ their menus.

(B) They're _____ tea.

(C) They're _____ _____
the menu.

(D) They're _____ dinner.

 ### Now You Try!

🔄 CheckLink 🎧 DL 027 〜 028 💿 CD1-27 〜 💿 CD1-28

写真を描写する4つの音声を聞いて、最も適切なものを選びましょう。

❶ Ⓐ Ⓑ Ⓒ Ⓓ

❷ Ⓐ Ⓑ Ⓒ Ⓓ

Part 2　Question-Response 【応答問題】

通常は Yes か No で答える疑問文に対して、それ以外で答える場合もあります。単純に Yes か No で始まる応答を選ばないように気をつけましょう。

Warming Up
CheckLink　DL 029 ~ 030　CD1-29 ~ CD1-30

音声を聞いて空所の語句を書き取り、質問に対する最も適切な応答を選びましょう。

1. Are you ready to order?

(A) No, _____ _____.

(B) No, I _____.

(C) Not _____.

2. Do you have a reservation?

(A) Yes, _____ is Tom Brown.

(B) No, it's _____.

(C) Very _____.

Now You Try!
CheckLink　DL 031 ~ 034　CD1-31 ~ CD1-34

質問とそれに対する 3 つの応答を聞いて、最も適切なものを選びましょう。

1. Ⓐ Ⓑ Ⓒ　　**2.** Ⓐ Ⓑ Ⓒ　　**3.** Ⓐ Ⓑ Ⓒ　　**4.** Ⓐ Ⓑ Ⓒ

Part 3　Conversations 【会話問題】

質問は基本的に会話に登場した順番に出題されます。このことを頭に入れて、できるだけ会話の流れについていきましょう。

Warming Up
CheckLink　DL 035 ~ 036　CD1-35 ~ CD1-36

音声を聞いて空所の語句を書き取り、質問に対する最も適切な答えを選びましょう。

> **W:** Where do you want to go for dinner on [1]_____?
>
> **M:** How about the new [2]_____ restaurant?
>
> **W:** That sounds good, but I heard it's very [3]_____ on [4]_____.
>
> **M:** OK, I'll [5]_____ them now and make a reservation.

1. When will the speakers go out for dinner?

(A) Tonight　　(B) On Thursday　　(C) On Friday　　(D) On Saturday

2. What restaurant does the man suggest?

(A) A Chinese restaurant　　　(B) A French restaurant

(C) A Japanese restaurant　　　(D) An Italian restaurant

3. What will the man do next?

(A) Make a phone call　　　(B) Check his schedule

(C) Look for another restaurant　　　(D) Suggest a different day

Now You Try!

CheckLink DL 037 ~ 040 CD1-37 ~ CD1-40

会話を聞いて、質問に対する最も適切な答えを選びましょう。

Conversation 1

1. Where does the woman work?
   - (A) At a hotel
   - (B) At a station
   - (C) At a department store
   - (D) At a restaurant

2. What does the man want to do?
   - (A) Buy a table
   - (B) Order a meal
   - (C) Look at the menu
   - (D) Make a reservation

3. What does the man request?
   - (A) A table at the back
   - (B) A table in the corner
   - (C) A table outside
   - (D) A table near a window

Conversation 2

4. What does the man order?
   - (A) Pasta
   - (B) Fried chicken
   - (C) A steak
   - (D) Fish

5. Which dressing does the man order?
   - (A) French
   - (B) Italian
   - (C) Thousand Island
   - (D) Blue cheese

6. What will the woman bring first?
   - (A) Some bread
   - (B) A glass of wine
   - (C) Some water
   - (D) A salad

Part 4 Talks

【説明文問題】

たいていの場合、1問目の質問は "What is the speaker talking about?" のように、トーク全体に関するものです。キーワードを聞き取って全体のポイントをつかみましょう。

Warming Up

CheckLink DL 041 ~ 042 CD1-41 ~ CD1-42

音声を聞いて空所の語句を書き取り、質問に対する最も適切な答えを選びましょう。

Hello, this is Doris Williams calling. I have a ¹_____ for this ²_____ night at 8:00. I'd like to ³_____ it to ⁴_____ night at the same time. I'll call again ⁵_____ and ⁶_____ the reservation. Thank you.

NOTE I'd like to ... …したい

1. What is the speaker talking about?

   (A) Dinner specials   (B) Restaurant tables   (C) A menu   (D) A reservation

2. What does the speaker want to do?

(A) Have lunch

(B) Call a friend

(C) Change a schedule

(D) Cancel a reservation

3. What will the speaker do tomorrow?

(A) Call the restaurant

(B) Make a delivery

(C) Place an order

(D) Visit a restaurant

Now You Try!

 CheckLink  DL 043 ~ 046 CD1-43 ~ CD1-46

説明文を聞いて、質問に対する最も適切な答えを選びましょう。

Talk 1	Talk 2

1. What is the speaker talking about?

(A) A hotel

(B) A department store

(C) A restaurant

(D) A train station

4. Who most likely is the speaker?

(A) A food service worker

(B) A truck driver

(C) A cook

(D) A salesperson

NOTE most likely おそらく

2. Who will receive a gift card?

(A) All groups

(B) All families

(C) The first 50 customers

(D) All customers

5. What did the speaker receive?

(A) An order

(B) A letter

(C) A payment

(D) A schedule

3. What will all customers receive?

(A) A free pizza

(B) A 10% discount

(C) A free drink

(D) A free salad

6. What will take about an hour?

(A) Cleaning a room

(B) Going to a company

(C) Cooking food

(D) Preparing a room

Vocabulary Builder (B)

CheckLink　DL 047　CD1-47

次の 1 ～ 8 の意味に合うものを a ～ h から選びましょう。その後で、音声を聞いて答えを確認しましょう。

1. chef （　）　**2.** dish （　）　**3.** own （　）　**4.** available （　）

5. offer （　）　**6.** dessert （　）　**7.** excellent （　）　**8.** reasonable （　）

a. デザート	**b.** 手ごろな	**c.** 皿、料理	**d.** 申し出 (る)
e. シェフ、料理人	**f.** 素晴らしい	**g.** 空いている、手に入る	**h.** 所有する

Part 5　Sentence Completion　【短文穴埋め問題】

Part 5 では代名詞に関する問題がよく出題されます。いろんな種類の代名詞とその使い方を覚えておきましょう。

代名詞の種類

主格 「…は」	目的格 「…を」	所有格 「…の」	所有代名詞 「…のもの」	再帰代名詞 「…自身」
I	me	my	mine	myself
you	you	your	yours	yourself
he	him	his	his	himself
she	her	her	hers	herself
it	it	its	—	itself
we	us	our	ours	ourselves
you	you	your	yours	yourselves
they	them	their	theirs	themselves

代名詞の使い方

● 主格の代名詞は「動詞の主語」として使われます。
　I like basketball.

● 目的格の代名詞は「動詞や前置詞の目的となる語」として使われます。
　*Ken called **me** last week. / Please give this book to **her**.*

● 所有格は名詞の前に置いて所有を表します。
　*Bob is washing **his** car.*

● 所有代名詞は前に出てきたものの代わりに使ったり、of の後ろに使ったりします。
　*"Is this Jane's pencil case?"　"No, it's **mine**."* (=No, it's **my pencil case**.)
　Susan is my friend. = *Susan is a friend of **mine**.*

● 再帰代名詞は目的語が主語と同じ場合に使われます。
　*Jane hurt **herself**.* (Jane=herself)
　*We enjoyed **ourselves** at the concert.* (We=ourselves)

Warming Up

CheckLink

正しい選択肢を選び、文を完成させましょう。

1. (**a.** He   **b.** They) are from England.
2. I see (**a.** she   **b.** her) every Monday.
3. That's (**a.** my   **b.** me) coat.
4. Bob is a friend of (**a.** ours   **b.** us).

Now You Try!

CheckLink

4 つの選択肢から最も適切なものを選び、文を完成させましょう。

1. ------- don't need a reservation for Pietro's Pizza.
   (A) You   (B) Your   (C) Yours   (D) Yourself

2. The chef cooked a special dinner for -------.
   (A) we   (B) our   (C) us   (D) ours

3. Bob Flemming is selling ------- seafood restaurant.
   (A) he   (B) his   (C) him   (D) himself

4. Mrs. Rogers bakes fresh pies, and her customers love -------.
   (A) they   (B) them   (C) their   (D) theirs

5. The Sunny Café owners will open ------- shop in Seattle.
   (A) they   (B) them   (C) their   (D) themselves

6. Mary owns the restaurant with a friend of -------.
   (A) she   (B) her   (C) hers   (D) herself

7. Customers enjoyed ------- at the Fireside Restaurant.
   (A) they   (B) their   (C) them   (D) themselves

8. Barney's Kitchen has a great menu for couples and ------- children.
   (A) they   (B) their   (C) them   (D) theirs

Part 6 | Text Completion 【長文穴埋め問題】

空所のある文だけでは選択肢の代名詞を絞りきれない場合、前の文を読んで、どの代名詞が当てはまるか考えましょう。

Warming Up
CheckLink

正しい選択肢を選び、文を完成させましょう。

1. Toru Kawasaki is our new chef. (**a.** He   **b.** We) worked in Tokyo and London.

2. Mr. and Mrs. Nelson have a dinner reservation for 7:00. Please give (**a.** her **b.** them) a table by the window.

3. Burger Barn offers a special birthday party plan. Call (**a.** him   **b.** us) at 555-0123 for more information.

4. Blueleaf Café has a private room for 10-12 people. (**a.** It's   **b.** They're) perfect for parties.

Now You Try!
CheckLink

4 つの選択肢から最も適切なものを選び、文を完成させましょう。

Questions 1–4 refer to the following article.

I recently -------- Ricky's Diner. It was a small place, and it was warm and friendly. The
     1.

waiter was very nice to --------. I ordered fish and chips. For dessert, I -------- a piece
       2.   **3.**

of cheesecake. Everything was excellent, and the price was very reasonable. --------.
                        4.

1. (A) called   (B) visited   (C) cleaned   (D) moved

2. (A) I   (B) my   (C) me   (D) mine

3. (A) have   (B) am having   (C) will have   (D) had

4. (A) I also ordered a large cola.   (B) It was on the table.
   (C) It was only $12.   (D) I had lunch at noon.

Part 7　Reading Comprehension　【読解問題】

TOEICで出題される質問を理解して、どんな情報を探せばよいのかを知ることは重要です。まずはWho、What、Where、When、Whyで始まる質問に慣れましょう。

Warming Up

次の 1~5 の日本語を英語の疑問文にしてみましょう。

1. Jack Smith とは誰ですか。　_____

2. Jack は何を尋ねましたか。　_____

3. Jack はどこで働いていますか。　_____

4. Jack の誕生日はいつですか。　_____

5. Jack はなぜ電話をかけましたか。　_____

Now You Try!

 CheckLink

文書を読んで、設問に対する最も適切な答えを選びましょう。

Questions 1–2 refer to the following advertisement.

Becky's Bistro
New Breakfast Buffet Starts on February 14!

Food
Bacon, sausages, eggs, French toast, pancakes and fresh fruit

Drinks
Fruit juices, milk, coffee and tea

Price: $16

The buffet will be available from 7 to 11 A.M. on Saturdays and Sundays.
*Buffet customers must come before 10:30.

NOTE buffet ビュッフェ（立食形式の食事）

1. What is the advertisement for?
   (A) A supermarket　　　　　(B) A fruit shop
   (C) A hotel　　　　　　　　(D) A restaurant

2. When is the buffet available?

(A) Monday to Friday

(B) On weekends

(C) On holidays

(D) On February 13

Questions 3–4 refer to the following text-message chain.

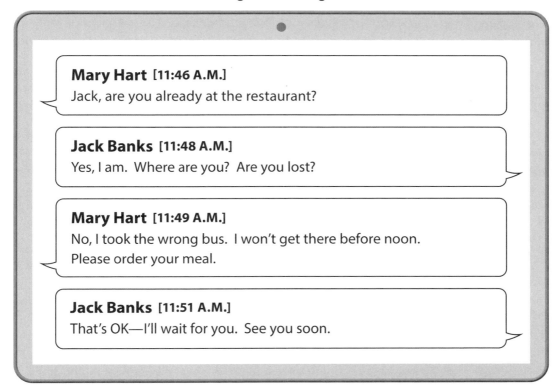

Mary Hart [11:46 A.M.]
Jack, are you already at the restaurant?

Jack Banks [11:48 A.M.]
Yes, I am. Where are you? Are you lost?

Mary Hart [11:49 A.M.]
No, I took the wrong bus. I won't get there before noon.
Please order your meal.

Jack Banks [11:51 A.M.]
That's OK—I'll wait for you. See you soon.

3. Why is Ms. Hart late?

(A) She got up late.

(B) She got on the wrong bus.

(C) Her train is late.

(D) She cannot find the restaurant.

4. At 11:51 A.M., what does Mr. Banks mean when he writes, "That's OK—I'll wait for you"?

(A) He will meet Ms. Hart at the train station.

(B) He will not order yet.

(C) He will look at the menu.

(D) He will go to a different restaurant.

Unit 3 Daily Life

トピック　日常生活　文法　形容詞

Vocabulary Builder A

CheckLink　DL 048　CD1-48

次の 1 ～ 8 の意味に合うものを a ～ h から選びましょう。その後で、音声を聞いて答えを確認しましょう。

1. exercise (　　)　**2.** clothes (　　)　**3.** electricity (　　)　**4.** bill (　　)

5. pharmacy (　　)　**6.** appointment (　　)　**7.** clinic (　　)　**8.** medicine (　　)

a. 電気	**b.** 薬	**c.** 予約、約束	**d.** 運動（する）
e. 請求書	**f.** 薬局	**g.** 診療所	**h.** 洋服

Part 1　Photographs

【写真描写問題】

3 人以上の人物の写真は、"They're" や "The men are" "The women are" で始まることがあります。その場合、人物たちの全体の動作に注目しましょう。

■ Warming Up

CheckLink　DL 049　CD1-49

音声を聞いて空所の語句を書き取り、写真を最も適切に描写しているものを選びましょう。

(A) They're _____ their legs.

(B) They're _____ their arms.

(C) They're _____ together.

(D) They're _____ their shoulders.

■ Now You Try!

CheckLink　DL 050 ～ 051　CD1-50 ～ CD1-51

写真を描写する 4 つの音声を聞いて、最も適切なものを選びましょう。

❶

Ⓐ Ⓑ Ⓒ Ⓓ

❷

Ⓐ Ⓑ Ⓒ Ⓓ

Part 2 Question-Response 【応答問題】

Yes か No で答える疑問文に対して、応答がすべて Yes か No で始まっていないこともあります。このような答え方を考える練習をしましょう。

Warming Up   CheckLink   DL 052 ~ 053   CD1-52 ~ CD1-53

音声を聞いて空所の語句を書き取り、質問に対する最も適切な応答を選びましょう。

1. Is the park far?

(A) It's near the _____.

(B) A _____ one.

(C) People are _____.

2. Are you enjoying your classes?

(A) In my _____.

(B) I have _____.

(C) Most of _____.

Now You Try!   CheckLink   DL 054 ~ 057   CD1-54 ~ CD1-57

質問とそれに対する 3 つの応答を聞いて、最も適切なものを選びましょう。

1. Ⓐ Ⓑ Ⓒ   **2.** Ⓐ Ⓑ Ⓒ   **3.** Ⓐ Ⓑ Ⓒ   **4.** Ⓐ Ⓑ Ⓒ

Part 3 Conversations 【会話問題】

2 問目と 3 問目の質問ではたいてい具体的なことについて問われます。会話のトピックとどのような関係があるのかに注意しながら、具体的な情報を聞き取るようにしましょう。

Warming Up   CheckLink   DL 058 ~ 059   CD1-58 ~ CD1-59

音声を聞いて空所の語句を書き取り、質問に対する最も適切な答えを選びましょう。

> **M:** Hi. I [1]_____ this book yesterday, but it doesn't have some [2]_____.
>
> **W:** I'm sorry to hear that. Let me check my [3]_____. ... Yes, we have another [4]_____. Please wait here. I will [5]_____ it for you.

1. Where are the speakers?

(A) In a clinic   (B) In a library   (C) In a pharmacy   (D) At a restaurant

2. Why does the man talk to the woman?

(A) He needs a receipt.   (B) He is looking for something.

(C) He wants advice.   (D) He has a problem.

3. What will the woman do next?

(A) Send an e-mail   (B) Make a copy   (C) Look for a book   (D) Order a book

31

Now You Try!

CheckLink DL 060 ~ 063 CD1-60 ~ CD1-63

会話を聞いて、質問に対する最も適切な答えを選びましょう。

Conversation 1

1. Where are the speakers?
   (A) In a post office
   (B) In a bakery
   (C) In a bank
   (D) In a pharmacy

2. What is the man's problem?
   (A) The weight
   (B) The address
   (C) The price
   (D) The size

3. How will the man send the package?
   (A) By ship
   (B) By train
   (C) By truck
   (D) By airplane

Conversation 2

4. What are the speakers talking about?
   (A) The price of heating
   (B) Their new air conditioner
   (C) A broken machine
   (D) Their electricity bill

5. How was the weather last month?
   (A) Cold
   (B) Rainy
   (C) Hot
   (D) Warm

6. What will the man do?
   (A) Clean a filter
   (B) Call an electricity company
   (C) Order a new air conditioner
   (D) Read a manual

Part 4 Talks   【説明文問題】

最後の質問では、"What will the man do next?" のように、次に起こることについて問われることがよくあります。トークの最後に正解のヒントがあるかもしれないので、注意して聞きましょう。

Warming Up

CheckLink DL 064 ~ 065 CD1-64 ~ CD1-65

音声を聞いて空所の語句を書き取り、質問に対する最も適切な答えを選びましょう。

Thank you for calling Stylists Hair Salon. We are unable to ¹_____ your call right now. Our regular hours are from ²_____ to ³_____ Tuesday to Friday, and ⁴_____ to ⁵_____ Saturday and Sunday. Please ⁶_____ a message. Thank you.

1. What time does Stylists Hair Salon open on Thursday?

(A) 8 A.M.   (B) 9 A.M.   (C) 10 A.M.   (D) 11 A.M.

2. What time does Stylists Hair Salon close on weekends?

(A) 4 P.M.   (B) 5 P.M.   (C) 6 P.M.   (D) 7 P.M.

3. What will the listener do next?

(A) Wait 1 minute   (B) Press "1"   (C) Call again later   (D) Leave a message

Now You Try!

 CheckLink  DL 066 ~ 069   CD1-66 ~ CD1-69

説明文を聞いて、質問に対する最も適切な答えを選びましょう。

Talk 1

1. What is the message about?

(A) A computer problem
(B) An appointment
(C) Clinic hours
(D) Some medicine

2. What is the clinic waiting for?

(A) A doctor
(B) A machine
(C) A bed
(D) Test results

3. What will the speaker do on Monday?

(A) Prepare a room
(B) Call Mrs. Barton
(C) Send a package
(D) Visit a hospital

Talk 2

4. What is the announcement about?

(A) Home fires
(B) City events
(C) New houses
(D) A new department store

5. Where do half of these accidents start?

(A) In the kitchen
(B) In the living room
(C) On the streets
(D) In the elevator

6. What will listeners probably do next?

(A) Buy some items
(B) Exercise together
(C) Clean their kitchen
(D) Look at a Web site

Vocabulary Builder　B

CheckLink　DL 070　CD1-70

次の 1 ～ 8 の意味に合うものを a ～ h から選びましょう。その後で、音声を聞いて答えを確認しましょう。

1. public（　　）　　**2.** library（　　）　　**3.** join（　　）　　**4.** membership（　　）

5. follow（　　）　　**6.** trash（　　）　　**7.** reduce（　　）　　**8.** renew（　　）

a. 会員（資格）	**b.** 図書館	**c.** ゴミ	**d.** 公共の、公の
e. 更新する	**f.** 加わる、参加する	**g.** 減らす	**h.** 従う

Part 5　Sentence Completion　　【短文穴埋め問題】

文の中で形容詞が来る位置を理解するとともに、できるだけたくさんの形容詞を覚えて見分けられるようにしましょう。

形容詞の使い方

● 形容詞は名詞を説明するのに使います。

形容詞＋名詞	be 動詞＋形容詞	一般動詞＋形容詞
*They have a **big** house.* *Bob is a **kind old** man.*	*The flowers are **beautiful**.* *Today is **warm** and **sunny**.*	*The bread smells **good**.* *Linda looks **cold**.*

形容詞の見分け方

● 単語の終わりの形から形容詞を見分けることができます。

port**able**　　invis**ible**　　internation**al**　　help**ful**　　care**less**　　artist**ic**　　mag**ical**

danger**ous**　　act**ive**　　health**y**

Warming Up

日本語の意味に合うように、空所を埋めて英語の形容詞を書きましょう。

1. 有名な：fam＿＿＿＿　　　　　　　**5.** スパイシーな：spic＿＿＿＿

2. 慎重な：care＿＿＿＿　　　　　　　**6.** 信じられない：unbeliev＿＿＿＿

3. 役に立たない：use＿＿＿＿　　　　　**7.** 音楽の：mus＿＿＿＿

4. 前向きな：posit＿＿＿＿　　　　　　**8.** 責任のある：respons＿＿＿＿

Now You Try!

CheckLink

4 つの選択肢から最も適切な選択肢を選び、文を完成させましょう。

1. This is a -------- area of the city.
   (A) fashionably　(B) fashion　(C) fashionable　(D) fashions

2. The Sheldon Public Library is a -------- place.
   (A) wonder　(B) wondered　(C) wonderful　(D) wonderfully

3. Our gas bill was -------- last month.
   (A) expense　(B) expensive　(C) expensively　(D) expensiveness

4. Buses are usually crowded on -------- days.
   (A) rain　(B) rains　(C) rained　(D) rainy

5. Mrs. Taylor grows vegetables in her -------- garden.
   (A) beautiful　(B) beautifully　(C) beautify　(D) beauty

6. All of the benches in the park have -------- designs.
   (A) original　(B) originally　(C) origin　(D) originating

7. The price of food is very -------- right now.
   (A) reason　(B) reasonable　(C) reasoning　(D) reasons

8. The city is making a -------- plan for the downtown area.
   (A) create　(B) creation　(C) creatively　(D) creative

Part 6 Text Completion 【長文穴埋め問題】

代名詞の所有格 (p.25) は名詞の前に置いて形容詞的に使います。また、所有代名詞は「…のもの」という意味を表します。空所のある文の前に登場している人やものを探すことで、どの代名詞を入れればよいかがわかります。

Warming Up
CheckLink

正しい選択肢を選び、文を完成させましょう。

1. John's train was 10 minutes late this morning. (**a.** His   **b.** Mine) was also late.

2. Please visit our Web site for information about city buses. (**a.** Its   **b.** Their) routes will change on September 1.

3. The Cornwall Library shows free movies on Sundays. (**a.** Its   **b.** My) theater room has seats for 50 people.

4. My wife and I joined the Q-City Fitness Club. My membership was $1,000, but (**a.** hers   **b.** theirs) was only $800.

Now You Try!
CheckLink

4 つの選択肢から最も適切な選択肢を選び、文を完成させましょう。

Questions 1–4 refer to the following instructions.

Please follow these simple ------- for trash collection in Royce City.
　　　　　　　　　　　　　　1.

1. Put ------- trash outside before 8 A.M.
　　　　2.

2. Use the blue container for burnable items. Use the green container for unburnable items such as glass and plastic.

3. -------. They are not -------. They belong to Royce City.
　　3.　　　　　　**4.**

LET'S KEEP OUR CITY CLEAN.

NOTES collection 収集 container 容器、コンテナ burnable 燃やせる belong to ... …に所属する

1. (A) rules   (B) words   (C) tools   (D) problems

2. (A) its   (B) our   (C) their   (D) your

3. (A) Keep your house clean.   (B) Do not move the containers.
   (C) Try to reduce your trash.   (D) Check the holiday schedule.

4. (A) mine   (B) ours   (C) yours   (D) theirs

Part 7 Reading Comprehension 【読解問題】

Part 7でよく出題される質問を知っておきましょう。質問の意味をすぐに理解できれば、回答に多くの時間をかけることができます。

Warming Up

次の 1~4 の質問の意味を a~d から選びましょう。

1. What is the purpose of …?   [   ]
2. What is the … mainly about?   [   ]
3. What is true about…?   [   ]
4. What is indicated about …?   [   ]

a. …は主に何についてですか
b. …について正しいのは何ですか
c. …の目的は何ですか
d. …について何が示されていますか

Now You Try!

文書を読んで、設問に対する最も適切な答えを選びましょう。

Questions 1–2 refer to the following letter.

December 23

Dear Ms.Kim,

We recommend that you have dental check-ups twice a year. Your only check-up this year was on May 23. That was seven months ago. Please call our office at 555-4567 and make an appointment.

Yours truly,

Park Avenue Dental Clinic

NOTES recommend 勧める check-up 検査、検診

1. What is the letter mainly about?

   (A) A payment   (B) A check-up   (C) An appointment   (D) A new machine

2. What is true about Ms. Kim?

   (A) She had a check-up on December 23.
   (B) She had two check-ups this year.
   (C) She had a check-up two months ago.
   (D) She had a check-up in May.

Questions 3–4 refer to the following e-mail.

To:	Jim Suzuki
From:	Ace Tennis Club
Date:	May 15
Subject:	Membership renewal

Dear Mr. Suzuki,

Thank you for coming to our tennis club for 15 years! Your membership ends at the end of next month. Renew before July 1 and you will receive a 10% discount.

For more information, call us or visit our Web site. Thank you.

Best regards,
Ace Tennis Club

3. What is the e-mail mainly about?
   (A) Tennis lessons
   (B) A new tennis club
   (C) A discount
   (D) A membership

4. When does Mr. Suzuki's membership end?
   (A) May 15
   (B) June 15
   (C) June 30
   (D) July 1

Unit 4 Travel

トピック 旅行) 文法 副詞

Vocabulary Builder (A)

CheckLink DL 071 CD1-71

次の1〜8の意味に合うものをa〜hから選びましょう。その後で、音声を聞いて答えを確認しましょう。

1. travel agent (　) **2.** book (　) **3.** luggage (　) **4.** fill out (　)

5. delay (　) **6.** passenger (　) **7.** due to (　) **8.** sightseeing (　)

a. 乗客	**b.** 遅延、遅らせる	**c.** 観光	**d.** 手荷物
e. 旅行業者	**f.** 記入する	**g.** 予約する	**h.** …が原因で

Part 1 Photographs 【写真描写問題】

人物が写っていない写真の場合、たいていは物に焦点が当てられています。"Some books are **on** the table." や "The car is **behind** the bus." のように、「場所を示す前置詞」を使って物の位置を表す文を聞いてみましょう。

Warming Up

CheckLink DL 072 CD1-72

音声を聞いて空所の語句を書き取り、写真を最も適切に描写しているものを選びましょう。

(A) The suitcase is _____ the bed.

(B) The suitcase is _____ the window.

(C) The suitcase is _____ the table.

(D) The suitcase is _____ the bed.

Now You Try!

CheckLink DL 073 ~ 074 CD1-73 ~ CD1-74

写真を描写する4つの音声を聞いて、最も適切なものを選びましょう。

❶

Ⓐ Ⓑ Ⓒ Ⓓ

❷

Ⓐ Ⓑ Ⓒ Ⓓ

39

Part 2　Question-Response 【応答問題】

Who で始まる疑問文は、Bill や Mr. Lee などの「人名」や、doctor などの「職業名」、roommate などの「関係」、the sales department などの「集団名」といったものが答えになります。このようなタイプの情報を注意して聞いて、質問の答えとなるか確認しましょう。

Warming Up　CheckLink　DL 075 ~ 076　CD1-75 ~ CD1-76

音声を聞いて空所の語句を書き取り、質問に対する最も適切な応答を選びましょう。

1. Who are you going to New York with?

(A) Linda's _____.

(B) Mike _____ there.

(C) Three of my _____.

2. Who planned your trip to Kyoto?

(A) Many beautiful _____.

(B) Karen _____.

(C) A good _____.

Now You Try!　CheckLink　DL 077 ~ 080　CD1-77 ~ CD1-80

質問とそれに対する 3 つの応答を聞いて、最も適切なものを選びましょう。

1. Ⓐ Ⓑ Ⓒ　　　**2.** Ⓐ Ⓑ Ⓒ　　　**3.** Ⓐ Ⓑ Ⓒ　　　**4.** Ⓐ Ⓑ Ⓒ

Part 3　Conversations 【会話問題】

会話に登場する人物の関係を理解することは重要です。場面が想像でき、会話についていきやすくなります。多くの場合、最初のやりとりを聞くことで関係が推測できます。

Warming Up　CheckLink　DL 081 ~ 082　CD1-81 ~ CD1-82

音声を聞いて空所の語句を書き取り、質問に対する最も適切な答えを選びましょう。

> **M:** Hello. I'd like to ¹_____ in, please. My name's Edward Jones. Here's my reservation ²_____.
>
> **W:** Thank you. You're ³_____ for two nights. This is your room ⁴_____ —Room 1207— and your ⁵_____ breakfast coupons. Enjoy your stay.

1. Where are the speakers?

(A) At a hotel　　(B) At a station　　(C) At an airport　　(D) At a restaurant

2. What does the man give to the woman?

(A) A credit card　　　　　　　(B) His passport

(C) A business card　　　　　　(D) His reservation number

3. What will the man receive?

(A) A map　　(B) Discount tickets　　(C) Free breakfast　　(D) A pamphlet

Now You Try!

CheckLink   DL 083 ~ 086   CD1-83 ~ CD1-86

会話を聞いて、質問に対する最も適切な答えを選びましょう。

Conversation 1

1. How long will the man be in New York?

(A) Two days

(B) Three days

(C) Four days

(D) Five days

2. What will the woman do for the man?

(A) Call the airport

(B) Contact his travel agent

(C) Change his travel schedule

(D) Arrange a tour

3. What will the man receive today?

(A) A phone call

(B) Tour information

(C) Tickets

(D) A schedule

Conversation 2

4. Where are the speakers?

(A) In a bank

(B) In a park

(C) In an airport

(D) In a department store

5. What is the woman's problem?

(A) She lost her passport.

(B) Her suitcase is broken.

(C) She cannot find her luggage.

(D) She does not have her ticket.

6. What will the woman do next?

(A) Fill out a card

(B) Wait for a taxi

(C) Look for her passport

(D) Open her suitcase

Part 4 Talks

【説明文問題】

"Please give me your answer tomorrow." のように、最後に聞き手に対して行動を取るように言うことがあります。最後の質問で問われることがあるので、ストーリーを意識して聞きましょう。

Warming Up

CheckLink   DL 087 ~ 088   CD1-87 ~ CD1-88

音声を聞いて空所の語句を書き取り、質問に対する最も適切な答えを選びましょう。

> This is your captain speaking. Due to [1]＿＿＿＿＿ winds and [2]＿＿＿＿＿ rain, we'll [3]＿＿＿＿＿ to Vancouver about 20 minutes [4]＿＿＿＿＿. We'll [5]＿＿＿＿＿ around 11:50 A.M. Please put on your [6]＿＿＿＿＿.

1. Where is the speaker?

(A) On an airplane   (B) On a bus   (C) On a ship   (D) On a train

2. What is the speaker talking about?

   (A) A company rule   (B) A computer problem

   (C) The reason for a delay   (D) A city's history

3. What will listeners do?

   (A) Eat lunch   (B) Show their tickets

   (C) Get their luggage   (D) Put on their seatbelts

Now You Try!

 CheckLink  DL 089 ~ 092   CD1-89 ~ CD1-92

説明文を聞いて、質問に対する最も適切な答えを選びましょう。

| Talk 1 | Talk 2 |

1. What is the speaker talking about?

   (A) A boat tour

   (B) A walking tour

   (C) A bus tour

   (D) A shopping tour

4. Who is calling Mr. Jones?

   (A) His assistant

   (B) A hotel manager

   (C) A car rental agency

   (D) A travel agent

2. How long is the tour?

   (A) 1 hour

   (B) 1.5 hours

   (C) 2 hours

   (D) 2.5 hours

5. What will the man receive?

   (A) A receipt

   (B) An airplane ticket

   (C) An area map

   (D) A reservation number

3. What will the listeners do?

   (A) Wear their seatbelts

   (B) Take pictures

   (C) Ask questions

   (D) Buy some postcards

6. What will the man do at the airport?

   (A) Take a taxi

   (B) Get on a shuttle bus

   (C) Meet Ms. Trent

   (D) Pick up a rental car

Vocabulary Builder (B)

CheckLink DL 093 CD1-93

次の 1 ～ 8 の意味に合うものを a ～ h から選びましょう。その後で、音声を聞いて答えを確認しましょう。

1. arrive (　　)　　　**2.** depart (　　)　　　**3.** tourist (　　)　　　**4.** rate (　　)

5. departure (　　)　　**6.** arrival (　　)　　　**7.** flight (　　)　　　**8.** airline (　　)

a. 観光客	**b.** 航空会社	**c.** (飛行機の) 便	**d.** 料金
e. 出発する	**f.** 到着する	**g.** 到着	**h.** 出発

Part 5　Sentence Completion　【短文穴埋め問題】

副詞はいろいろなものに説明を加えることができます。また、さまざまな意味や働きがあるので慣れておきましょう。

副詞の使い方

● 副詞は動詞、形容詞、別の副詞について、さらに説明を加える場合に使います。また、副詞は最後がたいてい ly で終わっています。

動詞＋副詞	副詞＋形容詞	副詞＋副詞
I drive **carefully**. *She works* **hard**.	*The airport is* **usually** *crowded*. *The office is* **really** *quiet*.	*She writes* **very nicely**. *You eat* **too quickly**. *He sings* **so beautifully**.

● 副詞は特に以下のことを表す場合に重要です。

時	*I saw Mary* **today** / **yesterday**. // *He gets up* **early** / **late**.
様子	*She speaks* **softly** / **clearly**. // *He sings* **well** / **badly**.
場所	*The children are* **upstairs** / **outside**. // *Your phone is* **here** / **there**.
程度	*It's* **quite** / **very** *cold today*. // *The class is* **so** / **too** *difficult*.
頻度	*I* **always** / **usually** / **often** / **sometimes** / **rarely** / **never** *eat breakfast*.

Warming Up

CheckLink

正しい選択肢を選び、文を完成させましょう。

1. It snowed (**a.** heavy　　**b.** heavily) yesterday.

2. The crowd of people is moving very (**a.** slowly　　**b.** slow).

3. Paris is (**a.** amazing　　**b.** amazingly) beautiful at night.

4. She speaks English (**a.** perfectly　　**b.** perfect).

Now You Try!

⟳ CheckLink

4 つの選択肢から最も適切なものを選び、文を完成させましょう。

1. The airplane arrived ------- at the airport.
   (A) safely   (B) safe   (C) safeness   (D) safety

2. The weather was ------- fine for sightseeing.
   (A) perfect   (B) perfectly   (C) perfection   (D) perfected

3. From the hotel, you can walk ------- to the beach.
   (A) ease   (B) easiness   (C) easily   (D) easy

4. Please check Mr. Clark's travel schedule -------.
   (A) careful   (B) carefulness   (C) care   (D) carefully

5. The number of tourists goes up ------- in the summer.
   (A) greatness   (B) great   (C) greaten   (D) greatly

6. Shuttle buses to the airport leave -------.
   (A) regular   (B) regulate   (C) regularly   (D) regulation

7. All trains are running very ------- this morning.
   (A) smooth   (B) smoothen   (C) smoothness   (D) smoothly

8. The special tour to Hawaii sold out -------.
   (A) quickly   (B) quick   (C) quickness   (D) quicken

Part 6 Text Completion 【長文穴埋め問題】

名詞の前に置いて数や量を表す語句を覚えましょう。
- 数えられる名詞の単数形と使える ➡ each, every, another
- 数えられる名詞の複数形と使える ➡ both
- 数えられる名詞の複数形と数えられない名詞の両方と使える ➡ all
- 数えられる名詞と数えられない名詞の両方と使える ➡ any, other

Warming Up

CheckLink

正しい選択肢を選び、文を完成させましょう。

1. (**a.** Every   **b.** All) passengers should go to Gate 12 now.
2. (**a.** Each   **b.** Both) room in the hotel has a large balcony.
3. There aren't (**a.** any   **b.** every) seats available on Flight 3.
4. We took one tour in the morning and (**a.** both   **b.** another) tour at night.

Now You Try!

CheckLink

4 つの選択肢から最も適切なものを選び、文を完成させましょう。

Questions 1–4 refer to the following letter.

Dear Mr. Spicer,

Thank you for staying at the Bruxton Hotel last month. Now, ------- Bruxton Hotels
                                                                            1.
have Check-In Machines. ------- machine has a large screen. You can check in
                                      2.
and check out. You can also pay for your room and ------- your room key. For more
                                                             3.
information, visit our Web site. -------.
                                      4.

Sincerely yours,

Janet Foster
Customer Service Manager, Bruxton Hotel

1. (A) each   (B) every   (C) all   (D) another
2. (A) All   (B) Each   (C) Both   (D) Other
3. (A) receive   (B) open   (C) clear   (D) close
4. (A) We will open on May 15.   (B) Please stay with us again soon.
   (C) We need your home address.   (D) We are sorry for the trouble.

Part 7 Reading Comprehension 【読解問題】

「スキャニング」は特定の情報を見つけるために素早く読む方法です。特に、「日付」「時刻」「値段」など、簡単に見つかることが多いものを探すときに役に立ちます。探している情報が見つかるまで関係のない情報は飛ばしましょう。

Warming Up

次のお知らせをスキャニングして、できるだけ早く質問に答えてみましょう。

SPRINGTIME HIKING TOUR

The Echo Hills 3 km hiking tour will be held on Sunday, April 30. The hike will begin at 9 A.M. and end around 10 A.M.

Registration fee:
$10
Price includes an Echo Hills T-shirt!

---

1. ハイキングが行われる季節はいつですか。　_____

2. ハイキングは何時にスタートしますか。　_____

3. 参加費はいくらですか。　_____

4. 参加費には何が含まれますか。　_____

Now You Try!

CheckLink

文書を読んで、設問に対する最も適切な答えを選びましょう。

Questions 1–2 refer to the following travel schedule.

Travel Schedule for Walter Bannon

DEPARTING FLIGHT

Date	Departs	Airline	Departure	Gate	Arrives	Arrival
January 4	06:15	All American	Los Angeles	C14	14:25	New York

HOTEL

Check-In	Name	Address	City	Room	Check-Out
January 4	Grandeur	808 Ames Avenue	New York	1225	January 9

---

1. What time will Mr. Bannon leave for New York?

   (A) At 1:04   (B) At 6:15   (C) At 12:25   (D) At 14:25

2. How many nights will Mr. Bannon stay?

   (A) 4   (B) 5   (C) 6   (D) 7

Questions 3–4 refer to the following e-mail.

To:	Margaret Davis
From:	Tim Hudson
Date:	September 5
Subject:	Tour schedule

Dear Ms. Davis,

Thank you for booking our "Autumn in Canada" tour. We changed your schedule a little. You will visit Montreal first and Quebec City second. Your "Standard" room is now a "Deluxe" room, but the price is the same. Enjoy the tour!

Yours sincerely,

Tim Hudson, Maple-A Travel

3. What is the e-mail mainly about?

   (A) A tour price

   (B) A tour guide

   (C) A tour bus

   (D) A tour schedule

4. What is indicated about the tour?

   (A) It happens in the summer.

   (B) It has a new schedule.

   (C) It will begin in Quebec City.

   (D) The price changed.

Unit 5 Entertainment

トピック　エンタテインメント ┃ 文 法　時制（現在・過去・未来）

Vocabulary Builder Ⓐ

CheckLink 　DL 094 　CD2-02

次の 1 〜 8 の意味に合うものを a 〜 h から選びましょう。その後で、音声を聞いて答えを確認しましょう。

1. amusement park （　） **2.** museum （　） **3.** draw （　） **4.** theater （　）

5. artwork （　） **6.** art gallery （　） **7.** stadium （　） **8.** performance （　）

a. 美術館、博物館	**b.** 公演、演奏	**c.** 劇場	**d.** 芸術作品
e. 画廊	**f.** 描く	**g.** スタジアム、競技場	**h.** 遊園地

Part 1 Photographs 【写真描写問題】

1 人の人物の動作を表す動詞と、その動詞の目的となる物の両方を注意して聞いて、写真を正しく表すものを選んでみましょう。

■ Warming Up

CheckLink 　DL 095 　CD2-03

音声を聞いて空所の語句を書き取り、写真を最も適切に描写しているものを選びましょう。

(A) She's _____ a dress.
(B) She's _____ a camera.
(C) She's _____ a ride.
(D) She's _____ a picture.

■ Now You Try!

CheckLink 　DL 096 ～ 097 　CD2-04 ～ CD2-05

写真を描写する 4 つの音声を聞いて、最も適切なものを選びましょう。

❶

Ⓐ Ⓑ Ⓒ Ⓓ

❷

Ⓐ Ⓑ Ⓒ Ⓓ

Part 2 Question-Response 【応答問題】

Whatで始まる疑問文は、"What is your name?" や "What did you do yesterday?" のように、ある特定の情報を尋ねます。また、"What color" "What time" "What kind" のように、「What ＋名詞」のかたちでよく使われます。どんな情報が問われているか注意して聞きましょう。

Warming Up CheckLink DL 098 ~ 099 CD2-06 ~ CD2-07

音声を聞いて空所の語句を書き取り、質問に対する最も適切な応答を選びましょう。

1. What time does the concert start?
   (A) Two _____.
   (B) At _____.
   (C) A _____ concert.

2. What kind of movie did you see?
   (A) Yes, it was very _____.
   (B) At the _____.
   (C) A _____.

Now You Try! CheckLink DL 100 ~ 103 CD2-08 ~ CD2-11

質問とそれに対する3つの応答を聞いて、最も適切なものを選びましょう。

1. (A) (B) (C)　　2. (A) (B) (C)　　3. (A) (B) (C)　　4. (A) (B) (C)

Part 3 Conversations 【会話問題】

表や地図、スケジュールなどの図表がある質問では、会話の内容と図表の情報をマッチさせる必要があります。Look at the graphic. で始まる質問に目を通しておきましょう。

Warming Up CheckLink DL 104 ~ 105 CD2-12 ~ CD2-13

音声を聞いて空所の語句を書き取り、質問に対する最も適切な答えを選びましょう。

M: Hello, I'd like one ¹_____, please.
W: That's ²_____ dollars.
M: Actually, I'm a ³_____ student. Here's my ID.
W: Then it's ⁴_____ dollars. But hurry, the ⁵_____ closes in half an hour.

Price A	$4
Price B	$11
Price C	$14
Price D	$25

1. What does the man buy?
   (A) A member's card　(B) A book　(C) A ticket　(D) A picture

2. Look at the graphic. Which price will the man pay?
   (A) Price A　(B) Price B　(C) Price C　(D) Price D

3. When does the museum close?
   (A) In 20 minutes　(B) In 30 minutes　(C) In 40 minutes　(D) In 1 hour

49

Now You Try!

CheckLink　DL 106 ~ 109　CD2-14 ~ CD2-17

会話を聞いて、質問に対する最も適切な答えを選びましょう。

Conversation 1

1. Where will the concerts be?

(A) At a stadium

(B) At a concert hall

(C) At an amusement park

(D) In a park

2. What will children receive?

(A) A drink

(B) A toy

(C) Ice cream

(D) A T-shirt

3. What will the man give the woman?

(A) A park map

(B) A concert schedule

(C) Free tickets

(D) A telephone number

Conversation 2

Cinerama Movie Schedule	
Cinema 1	*Green Peas* (comedy)
Cinema 2	*Alien Eyes* (science fiction)
Cinema 3	*Silent Walk* (mystery)
Cinema 4	*Dark Creatures* (horror)

4. When will the speakers go to a movie?

(A) Tonight　　　　(B) Tomorrow night

(C) On Saturday　　(D) On Sunday

5. Look at the graphic. Which movie will the speakers see?

(A) *Green Peas*　　(B) *Alien Eyes*

(C) *Silent Walk*　　(D) *Dark Creatures*

6. Where will the speakers meet?

(A) Inside the theater

(B) Near the ticket office

(C) At the woman's house

(D) In front of the theater

Part 4　Talks

【説明文問題】

"7 P.M." → "in the evening" のように、トークで登場した語句や表現が選択肢では言い換えられていることがあります。トークに登場した表現が選択肢にあるからといって、すぐに答えを選ばないようにしましょう。

Warming Up

CheckLink　DL 110 ~ 111　CD2-18 ~ CD2-19

音声を聞いて空所の語句を書き取り、質問に対する最も適切な答えを選びましょう。

Today's guest is ballet [1]＿＿＿＿＿＿ Yui Sano. Ms. Sano was [2]＿＿＿＿＿＿ in Tokyo. She [3]＿＿＿＿＿＿ to the United States at the age of three. The next year, she started [4]＿＿＿＿＿＿ ballet. She became a lead [5]＿＿＿＿＿＿ of the Rose Ballet Company in 2020. Ms. Sano, [6]＿＿＿＿＿＿ to the show.

1. Who most likely is the speaker?

(A) A doctor   (B) A shop owner   (C) A ballet teacher   (D) A talk show presenter

2. When did Ms. Sano begin her ballet studies?

(A) At age three   (B) At age four   (C) At age five   (D) At age six

3. How did Ms. Sano's life change in 2020?

(A) She changed companies.   (B) She moved to Japan.

(C) She became a main dancer.   (D) She opened a dance school.

Now You Try!

 CheckLink   DL 112 ~ 115   CD2-20 ~ CD2-23

説明文を聞いて、質問に対する最も適切な答えを選びましょう。

Talk 1

1. Where is the speaker?

(A) In a museum

(B) In a concert hall

(C) In an amusement park

(D) In a movie theater

2. Where can people eat and drink?

(A) In the balcony

(B) At the back of the hall

(C) In the lobby

(D) In the park

3. What will listeners do next?

(A) Take pictures

(B) Show their tickets

(C) Take off their hats

(D) Switch off their phones

Talk 2

4. Who is the man?

(A) A studio manager

(B) A cameraman

(C) A reporter

(D) A tour guide

5. What is *Gold Diamonds*?

(A) A movie studio

(B) Jewelry

(C) A popular movie

(D) An outdoor stage

6. What is behind the listeners?

(A) A coffee shop

(B) A ticket counter

(C) A gift shop

(D) An entrance

Vocabulary Builder Ⓑ

 CheckLink　 DL 116　◉ CD2-24

次の 1 ～ 8 の意味に合うものを a ～ h から選びましょう。その後で、音声を聞いて答えを確認しましょう。

1. orchestra（　　）　**2.** perform（　　）　**3.** painting（　　）　**4.** exhibit（　　）

5. famous（　　）　**6.** admission fee（　　）　**7.** review（　　）　**8.** culture（　　）

a. 入場料	**b.** 絵画	**c.** 有名な	**d.** 文化
e. 演奏する	**f.** オーケストラ	**g.** 評論、検討する	**h.** 展示（する）

Part 5 Sentence Completion 【短文穴埋め問題】

正しい時制を選ぶ問題では、時や頻度を表す表現を探しましょう。

現在時制

● 事実や一般的な真理、ずっと続くと思われることを述べる場合に使います。
*It **rains** a lot in London. / The Earth **is** round. / I **work** in a bank.*

● 習慣や何かが起こる頻度を述べる場合に使います。
*Ed **plays** tennis every Sunday. / He never **cooks**. / She **gets** up at 6 A.M. on weekdays.*

過去時制

● 過去の行動を述べる場合に使います。一緒によく使われる語句には、yesterday、last week、… ago などがあります。
*Shakespeare **wrote** Romeo and Juliet. / I **worked** hard last week. / We **went** to a concert three days ago.*

未来時制

● 未来の行動や予想される行動を述べる場合に使います。一緒によく使われる語句には、tomorrow、next month、in … minutes などがあります。
*It **will rain** tomorrow. / We **will travel** to Chicago next month. / I **will call** you in 30 minutes.*

Warming Up

（　　）内の動詞を正しい時制に変えて、文を完成させましょう。

1. Tom .... last night. (work)

2. Dinner .... ready soon. (be)

3. The bus .... in a few minutes. (arrive)

4. The sun .... in the east. (rise)

Now You Try!

CheckLink

4つの選択肢から最も適切な選択肢を選び、文を完成させましょう。

1. The new art exhibit ------- a week ago.
   (A) starts   (B) started   (C) will start   (D) start

2. Every year, the circus ------- to Devin Center.
   (A) comes   (B) come   (C) coming   (D) will come

3. Ted Walker ------- a talk about British culture next month.
   (A) give   (B) will give   (C) gave   (D) gives

4. People ------- an excellent dinner show last night.
   (A) enjoy   (B) enjoying   (C) will enjoy   (D) enjoyed

5. The city orchestra ------- a concert at Jefferson Hall tomorrow.
   (A) performs   (B) performed   (C) will perform   (D) performing

6. The museum now ------- a wonderful collection of French paintings.
   (A) has   (B) having   (C) will have   (D) had

7. Customers ------- the ticket prices for the concert in two weeks.
   (A) know   (B) knew   (C) will know   (D) knowing

8. Games between the two teams ------- usually very exciting.
   (A) are   (B) was   (C) will be   (D) is

Part 6　Text Completion　【長文穴埋め問題】

選択肢のすべての動詞の形が空所に当てはまりそうな場合は、前の文の動詞の形（時制）をもう一度よく見てみましょう。正しい答えを選ぶのに役立つ可能性があります。

Warming Up　CheckLink

正しい選択肢を選び、文を完成させましょう。

1. Justin Hawkins began his Asian tour last night. He (**a.** is performing **b.** performed) songs from his new album.

2. The Natural History Museum will close for the holidays. It (**a.** will reopen **b.** reopened) on January 5.

3. Last night's game between the Yankees and Red Socks was very long. It (**a.** ended **b.** will end) around 11 P.M.

4. The dancers are not on stage yet. First, they (**a.** warmed up **b.** will warm up) in the studio.

Now You Try!　CheckLink

4つの選択肢から最も適切な選択肢を選び、文を完成させましょう。

Questions 1–4 refer to the following letter.

Dear Ms. Bell,

Thank you for asking about group discounts. The admission fee for groups of 10 or ------- people is $7. Group discounts are NOT ------- on weekends and holidays.
　　　　1.　　　　　　　　　　　　　　　　　　　　　　**2.**
-------.
　3.

We are building a new Penguin Pool now. It ------- on June 15.
　　　　　　　　　　　　　　　　　　　4.

Sincerely,

Glen Campbell, Brock Valley Zoo

1. (A) more　(B) up　(C) plus　(D) higher

2. (A) ready　(B) available　(C) much　(D) true

3. (A) We're not open on holidays.　(B) We also have a gift shop.
   (C) The zoo is very crowded today.　(D) Please make a reservation for your group.

4. (A) opened　(B) open　(C) will open　(D) was opening

Part 7 Reading Comprehension 【読解問題】

「スキミング」は全体的な意味を見つけるために素早く読む方法です。文書の目的や何についての文章かを問う質問に答える際に役に立ちます。すべて読む必要はなく、たいてい見出しや最初の1〜2文を読めば十分です。

Warming Up

CheckLink

次の記事をスキミングして、質問に答えましょう。

The Peach Science Museum is a wonderful place for children aged 3 to 6 years old. Children will learn about water, light and many other things in interesting ways.

What is the article mainly about?（記事は主に何についてですか）

(A) Light and water　　(B) A museum for young children

Now You Try!

CheckLink

文書を読んで、設問に対する最も適切な答えを選びましょう。

Questions 1–2 refer to the following notice.

New Exhibit at the Dawson City Art Gallery

From March 6 to 14, the Dawson City Art Gallery will display works of famous artists from the city. There will be about 200 artworks, including paintings by Colin Wright. All items are for sale. You can also see and buy them online. The gallery is open every day from 11 A.M. to 6 P.M.

NOTE　including ... …を含む

1. What is the notice about?
   (A) The opening of a new art gallery
   (B) A visit by a famous artist
   (C) A new art exhibit
   (D) An online sale

2. What is true about Mr. Wright?
   (A) He does not paint anymore.　　(B) He lives in Dawson City.
   (C) He owns an art studio.　　(D) He will be at the gallery.

Questions 3–5 refer to the following review.

Album Review
-by Eddie Banks-

—May 18—

Singer-songwriter Stephanie Melville's new album *Tiny Dreams* is now on sale. It is the pop singer's first solo album. She left her band Puff Jam one year ago. The songs on the album are about her young daughter. "Little Mandy" is number 1 on the pop charts. I like everything about the album, especially Melville's beautiful singing voice.

3. What is the name of Stephanie Melville's new album?
   (A) Puff Jam
   (B) *Tiny Dreams*
   (C) Eddie Banks
   (D) "Little Mandy"

4. What is true about Ms. Melville?
   (A) She is a new artist.
   (B) She performs hip hop music.
   (C) She was in a band before.
   (D) She plays the guitar.

5. What are Ms. Melville's songs about?
   (A) Her childhood
   (B) Her dreams
   (C) Her travels
   (D) Her daughter

Unit 6 — News & Media

トピック ニュース＆メディア　　文法 進行形・現在完了形

Vocabulary Builder (A)

CheckLink 🎧 DL 117 ◎ CD2-25

次の 1 ～ 8 の意味に合うものを a ～ h から選びましょう。その後で、音声を聞いて答えを確認しましょう。

1. article (　　)　**2.** traffic (　　)　**3.** photographer (　　)　**4.** press conference (　　)

5. report (　　)　　　**6.** temperature (　　)　　**7.** weather (　　)　　**8.** cause (　　)

a. 記者会見	**b.** 写真家、カメラマン	**c.** 交通	**d.** 気温
e. 記事	**f.** 天気	**g.** 報道（する）	**h.** 原因、引き起こす

Part 1　Photographs　　　　【写真描写問題】

男女が 1 人ずつ写っている写真では、"A (The) man is …" "A (The) woman is …" "He's …" "She's …" と聞こえたら、その人物の動作に注目して文の後半を聞きましょう。

Warming Up

CheckLink 🎧 DL 118 ◎ CD2-26

音声を聞いて空所の語句を書き取り、写真を最も適切に描写しているものを選びましょう。

(A) She's _____ her legs.

(B) He's _____ _____ a hat.

(C) She's _____ a walk.

(D) He's _____ the newspaper.

Now You Try!

CheckLink 🎧 DL 119 ～ 120 ◎ CD2-27 ～ ◎ CD2-28

写真を描写する 4 つの音声を聞いて、最も適切なものを選びましょう。

❶

Ⓐ Ⓑ Ⓒ Ⓓ

❷

Ⓐ Ⓑ Ⓒ Ⓓ

Part 2 Question-Response 【応答問題】

When で始まる疑問文には、"at 2:00" "in the morning" "on Monday" のような「前置詞＋時を表す語句」や、"yesterday" "tomorrow" "… ago" "last week" "next month" のような語句で通常は答えます。When で始まる疑問文が聞こえたら、このような表現が来ることを予測しましょう。

Warming Up
CheckLink　DL 121 ~ 122　CD2-29 ~ CD2-30

音声を聞いて空所の語句を書き取り、質問に対する最も適切な応答を選びましょう。

1. When does the press conference begin?
   (A) _____ night.
   (B) On Channel _____.
   (C) At _____.

2. When did you hear about the new company?
   (A) In the _____.
   (B) On the 6 o'clock _____.
   (C) Next _____.

Now You Try!
CheckLink　DL 123 ~ 126　CD2-31 ~ CD2-34

質問とそれに対する3つの応答を聞いて、最も適切なものを選びましょう。

1. (A) (B) (C)　　2. (A) (B) (C)　　3. (A) (B) (C)　　4. (A) (B) (C)

Part 3 Conversations 【会話問題】

できれば、音声が流れる前に最初の質問に目を通してみましょう。何についての会話か、何を聞けばよいか、ヒントが得られます。

Warming Up
CheckLink　DL 127 ~ 128　CD2-35 ~ CD2-36

音声を聞いて空所の語句を書き取り、質問に対する最も適切な答えを選びましょう。

> W: Did you hear about the [1]_____ accident?
> M: Yes, I heard about it on the [2]_____. It was [3]_____ heavily, so the [4]_____ couldn't [5]_____ very well.
> W: Luckily, everyone is OK.

1. What news are the speakers talking about?
   (A) A live concert　　　　　　(B) A car accident
   (C) A baseball game　　　　　(D) A press conference

2. How did the man learn about the news?
   (A) On the radio　(B) On television　(C) In the newspaper　(D) From a friend

3. What was the cause of the accident?
   (A) A big noise　(B) A heavy weight　(C) A low temperature　(D) A heavy rain

Now You Try!

CheckLink DL 129 ~ 132 CD2-37 ~ CD2-40

会話を聞いて、質問に対する最も適切な答えを選びましょう。

Conversation 1

1. What does the woman think about social media?

(A) She believes it.

(B) She does not trust it.

(C) She does not have time for it.

(D) She likes most of the articles.

2. Why does the woman like *News of the World*?

(A) It has a history of over 100 years.

(B) The reports are short.

(C) It is a large company.

(D) It is fair.

3. What can the man get for free?

(A) A calendar

(B) Online articles

(C) A poster

(D) A book

Conversation 2

4. What is the man writing about?

(A) A movie director

(B) A press conference

(C) A new art gallery

(D) A traffic accident

5. What did the man do in the morning?

(A) He spoke with his assistant.

(B) He took some pictures.

(C) He attended a meeting.

(D) He interviewed a gallery worker.

6. What does the woman want to do?

(A) Move her desk

(B) Hear about the news

(C) Leave the office

(D) Put the article on the first page

Part 4 Talks

【説明文問題】

Part 4 ではラジオのニュース放送が出題されることがあります。交通情報や天気予報などでよく使われる語句や表現を覚えておくと聞き取りやすくなります。

Warming Up

CheckLink DL 133 ~ 134 CD2-41 ~ CD2-42

音声を聞いて空所の語句を書き取り、質問に対する最も適切な答えを選びましょう。

This is Amanda Clark with your 11 P.M. [1] _____ report. It'll be [2] _____ tonight with a low of [3] _____ degrees centigrade. Tomorrow will be [4] _____ with a high of [5] _____ degrees centigrade. But there will be heavy [6] _____ throughout most of the day. Please be careful.

NOTE ... degrees centigrade セ氏…℃

1. What is the speaker talking about?

(A) Traffic information

(B) Weather information

(C) Sports news

(D) Business news

2. What will be the highest temperature tomorrow?

(A) 11°C   (B) 15°C   (C) 20°C   (D) 25°C

3. What will the weather be tomorrow?

(A) Sunny   (B) Cloudy   (C) Rainy   (D) Windy

🔲 Now You Try!   ⟳CheckLink   🎧 DL 135 ~ 138   ◎ CD2-43 ~ ◎ CD2-46

説明文を聞いて、質問に対する最も適切な答えを選びましょう。

Talk 1

1. What is the main topic of the news?

(A) An outdoor concert

(B) A driver

(C) An accident

(D) City workers

2. What will happen in several hours?

(A) Workers will begin their work.

(B) A train will restart.

(C) A city park will close.

(D) A road will reopen.

3. What will listeners do?

(A) Use Maple Street

(B) Drive carefully

(C) Bring an umbrella

(D) Check a Web site

Talk 2

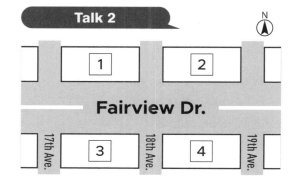

4. What is the speaker talking about?

(A) A concert hall

(B) A shopping center

(C) A city library

(D) A sports ground

5. Look at the graphic. Where will the new building be?

(A) 1   (B) 2   (C) 3   (D) 4

6. What will the building become?

(A) A public library

(B) A city museum

(C) A movie theater

(D) The home of a sports team

Vocabulary Builder (B)

CheckLink DL 139 CD2-47

次の１〜８の意味に合うものを a〜h から選びましょう。その後で、音声を聞いて答えを確認しましょう。

1. heavy snow (　) **2.** volunteer (　) **3.** local (　) **4.** announce (　)

5. reporter (　) **6.** invite (　) **7.** raise (　) **8.** host (　)

a. 記者	**b.** 司会者、主催する	**c.** 発表する	**d.** 地元の
e. 大雪	**f.** 上げる	**g.** 招待する	**h.** ボランティア、志願する

Part 5 Sentence Completion 【短文穴埋め問題】

動詞の時制の中には be 動詞や have を使って作るものもあります。こうした時制の使い方に慣れておきましょう。

現在進行形 〈be動詞（am / is / are）＋動詞のing形〉

● 話している時点で進行中の行動や出来事を述べる場合に使います。
*I **am studying** now. / She **is cooking** dinner. / They **are watching** TV.*

● また、一時的な状態や行動を述べる場合にも使います。
*He **is staying** with his aunt right now. / They **are studying** hard these days.*

過去進行形 〈be動詞の過去形（was / were）＋動詞のing形〉

● 過去のある時点で進行していた行動や出来事を述べる場合に使います。
*I **was having** dinner then. / At this time last week, we **were skiing** in France.*

現在完了 〈have（has）＋動詞の過去分詞〉

● 過去に始まって現在も続いていることを述べる場合に使います。
*He **has lived** in Tokyo since 2010. / They **have had** the same car for 20 years.*

● また、現在までの経験を述べる場合にも使います。
*She **has been** to Disneyland a few times. / I **have** never **seen** this movie.*

Warming Up

CheckLink

正しい選択肢を選び、文を完成させましょう。

1. He (**a.** watches **b.** is watching) the news now.

2. I (**a.** am **b.** was) writing a report then.

3. They (**a.** have **b.** were) visited Japan many times.

4. They (**a.** are **b.** have been) friends since high school.

61

Now You Try!

CheckLink

4 つの選択肢から最も適切なものを選び、文を完成させましょう。

1. KBC Television ------- on a forest fire now.
   (A) report   (B) was reporting   (C) is reporting   (D) reported

2. Last night, heavy snow ------- most roads in the city.
   (A) is blocking   (B) have blocked   (C) has blocked   (D) was blocking

3. Susan Baylor ------- a news reporter since 2010.
   (A) is   (B) has been   (C) was   (D) have been

4. Right now, the president ------- at a press conference.
   (A) speak   (B) is speaking   (C) has spoken   (D) was speaking

5. Dan Miller ------- articles for 30 years.
   (A) is writing   (B) are writing   (C) has written   (D) have written

6. Fifty reporters ------- outside the actor's house yesterday.
   (A) wait   (B) were waiting   (C) have waited   (D) are waiting

7. Christine Kline ------- for a local radio station then.
   (A) works   (B) is working   (C) has worked   (D) was working

8. The reporter ------- abroad several times for press conferences.
   (A) has traveled   (B) travel   (C) were traveling   (D) have traveled

Part 6 | Text Completion 【長文穴埋め問題】

選択肢のすべての動詞の形が空所に当てはまりそうで、前の文を見ても手がかりがつかめない場合は、後ろの文を見てみましょう。

Warming Up ⟳CheckLink

正しい選択肢を選び、文を完成させましょう。

1. Actors Meg Sims and Tom Knight (**a.** are spending   **b.** spent) their honeymoon in Hawaii. They will return to Los Angeles on Sunday.

2. James Dixon (**a.** will sign   **b.** signed) his new book at Mason's Bookstore. Many fans waited outside for three hours.

3. The *L.A. Daily Times* (**a.** will sell   **b.** was selling) a special edition. It will be available from April 1.

4. Craft Motors (**a.** will have   **b.** had) a press conference today. They announced the sale of the company to Bandy Auto.

Now You Try! ⟳CheckLink

4 つの選択肢から最も適切なものを選び、文を完成させましょう。

Questions 1–4 refer to the following article.

> Lonny's Foods announced today that they ------- all of their discount supermarkets.
> **1.**
> The stores will close on May 31. In 2010, they promised "quality food at -------
> **2.**
> prices." -------. However, in 2021, Lonny's raised their prices, and they ------- many
> **3.**   **4.**
> customers.

1. (A) close   (B) have closed   (C) will close   (D) closed

2. (A) low   (B) small   (C) high   (D) bottom

3. (A) They open at 8 A.M.   (B) In 2020, there were 45 stores.
   (C) They sell jeans and T-shirts.   (D) It is very popular now.

4. (A) bought   (B) found   (C) sold   (D) lost

Part 7　Reading Comprehension 【読解問題】

文書の「見出し」やEメールの「件名」を読むことで何についての文書かがわかり、どんな
タイプの情報が含まれているかを予測することができます。

■ Warming Up

CheckLink

次の 1～5 の見出しを最も適切に表しているものを a～e から選びましょう。

1. Johnny and the Boys Will Perform in Tokyo　[　]　**a.** スーパーマーケットのセール

2. Typhoon Causes Train Delays　[　]　**b.** コンサート

3. Bays Company buys Den Computer for $500 million　[　]　**c.** 求人

4. Save 20% on bread　[　]　**d.** 悪天候

5. Wanted: Assistant Sales Manager　[　]　**e.** 企業の買収

■ Now You Try!

CheckLink

文書を読んで、設問に対する最も適切な答えを選びましょう。

Questions 1–2 refer to the following article.

FIRES IN CALIFORNIA

San Francisco — Large forest fires are still burning in northern California. The area has been very hot and dry since the beginning of the month. Already 21 homes have burned. There is some good news, however — it will be cool and rainy next week.

1. What is the article mainly about?
   (A) Houses in California
   (B) A local event
   (C) Forest fires
   (D) A park near San Francisco

2. What will happen next week?
   (A) News reporters will come to California.
   (B) The weather will change.
   (C) A TV show host will invite local people to the show.
   (D) Some people will leave their homes.

Questions 3–5 refer to the following e-mail.

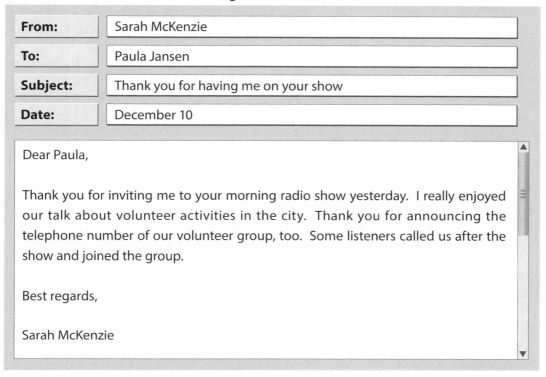

From:	Sarah McKenzie
To:	Paula Jansen
Subject:	Thank you for having me on your show
Date:	December 10

Dear Paula,

Thank you for inviting me to your morning radio show yesterday. I really enjoyed our talk about volunteer activities in the city. Thank you for announcing the telephone number of our volunteer group, too. Some listeners called us after the show and joined the group.

Best regards,

Sarah McKenzie

3. Why did Ms. McKenzie write the e-mail?
   (A) She wanted to invite Paula to an event.
   (B) She wanted to talk about volunteer activities.
   (C) She wanted to thank Paula.
   (D) She wanted to join a volunteer group.

4. Who most likely is Paula?
   (A) A teacher   (B) A doctor   (C) A volunteer   (D) A talk show host

5. What did some people do after the show?
   (A) They went to a party.   (B) They became volunteers.
   (C) They ordered a book.   (D) They called Paula.

Housing

Vocabulary Builder A

CheckLink DL 140 CD2-48

次の 1 ～ 8 の意味に合うものを a ～ h から選びましょう。その後で、音声を聞いて答えを確認しましょう。

1. floor plan ( )　　**2.** rent ( )　　**3.** real estate agent ( )　　**4.** replace ( )

5. estimate ( )　　**6.** neighborhood ( )　　**7.** plant ( )　　**8.** moving company ( )

a. 家賃、賃貸する	**b.** 近所	**c.** 引っ越し会社	**d.** 間取り図
e. 不動産業者	**f.** 取り替える	**g.** 見積もり、見積もる	**h.** 植える、植物

Part 1　Photographs

【写真描写問題】

3 人以上の人物が写っている場合、そのうちの 1 人だけの動作を述べることがあります。文の主語を注意して聞いて、その人物の動作に焦点を絞りましょう。

Warming Up

CheckLink DL 141 CD2-49

音声を聞いて空所の語句を書き取り、写真を最も適切に描写しているものを選びましょう。

(A) One of the men is _____ on the phone.

(B) One of the men is _____ a paper.

(C) A woman is _____ a photo.

(D) One of the men is _____ a sign.

Now You Try!

CheckLink DL 142 ~ 143 CD2-50 ~ CD2-51

写真を描写する 4 つの音声を聞いて、最も適切なものを選びましょう。

❶ Ⓐ Ⓑ Ⓒ Ⓓ

❷ Ⓐ Ⓑ Ⓒ Ⓓ

Part 2 Question-Response 【応答問題】

Whereで始まる疑問文には、"on the table" "under the bridge" "next to the bank"のように「前置詞＋場所を表す語句」で通常は答えます。Where で始まる疑問文が聞こえたら、このような表現が来ることを予測しましょう。

Warming Up CheckLink DL 144 ~ 145 CD2-52 ~ CD2-53

音声を聞いて空所の語句を書き取り、質問に対する最も適切な応答を選びましょう。

1. Where's your new apartment?
(A) Two _____.
(B) The building has 15 _____.
(C) _____ from Central Park.

2. Where are the floor plans?
(A) I'll _____ the floor.
(B) On the _____.
(C) I'll plant them in the _____.

Now You Try! CheckLink DL 146 ~ 149 CD2-54 ~ CD2-57

質問とそれに対する 3 つの応答を聞いて、最も適切なものを選びましょう。

1. (A) (B) (C)   **2.** (A) (B) (C)   **3.** (A) (B) (C)   **4.** (A) (B) (C)

Part 3 Conversations 【会話問題】

会話を聞きながら質問を読むよりも、会話を聞くことに集中しましょう。そのほうが内容を最大限に理解でき、細かい点も記憶に残ります。

Warming Up CheckLink DL 150 ~ 151 CD2-58 ~ CD2-59

音声を聞いて空所の語句を書き取り、質問に対する最も適切な答えを選びましょう。

M: Where would you like this ¹_____?
W: Please put it in front of the ²_____ in the bedroom.
M: OK. And these ³_____?
W: They go in the ⁴_____. The table goes in the ⁵_____ room.

1. Who most likely is the man?
(A) A customer   (B) A doctor   (C) A moving company worker   (D) A musician

2. What will the man put in the bedroom?
(A) A chair   (B) A plant   (C) A sofa   (D) A bookcase

3. Where will the table go?
(A) In the kitchen   (B) In the office   (C) In the dining room   (D) In the living roon

67

▶ Now You Try!

CheckLink   DL 152 ~ 155   CD2-60 ~ CD2-63

会話を聞いて、質問に対する最も適切な答えを選びましょう。

Conversation 1

1. What is the conversation about?

(A) Pipes

(B) Wallpaper

(C) Windows

(D) A roof

2. What do we learn about the house?

(A) It is very large.

(B) It is over 30 years old.

(C) It has a unique design.

(D) It is for sale.

3. What will the man send the woman?

(A) A price for some work

(B) A catalog

(C) A work schedule

(D) A sample

Conversation 2

4. Where are the speakers?

(A) At a real estate agency

(B) At a department store

(C) At a bookstore

(D) At a school

5. What does the man want to do?

(A) Sell his home

(B) Buy a house

(C) Borrow some money

(D) Go to school

6. What will the woman do next?

(A) Talk to her manager

(B) Print a report

(C) Make an appointment   .

(D) Enter some data

Part 4 Talks   【説明文問題】

Part 4 では話し手が誰かを尋ねる問題がよく出ます。このタイプの質問に答えるために、さまざまな職業名を覚えておくようにしましょう。

▶ Warming Up

CheckLink   DL 156 ~ 157   CD2-64 ~ CD2-65

音声を聞いて空所の語句を書き取り、質問に対する最も適切な答えを選びましょう。

> Hello, I'm Don Stanley, [1] _____ of Stanley Movers. Are you looking for a good [2] _____ company? For 50 years, Stanley Movers has given [3] _____ service at [4] _____ prices. Now [5] _____ 40% on [6] _____ material. Call 555-6789 today.

1. Who is Don Stanley?

(A) A company president   (B) A driver   (C) A sales manager   (D) A trainer

2. What is Stanley Movers?

(A) A moving company   (B) A travel company

(C) A fitness company   (D) A taxi company

3. What can customers receive?

(A) A gift   (B) A discount   (C) A free rental car   (D) An upgrade

Now You Try!

 CheckLink  DL 158～161 CD2-66 ～ CD2-69

説明文を聞いて、質問に対する最も適切な答えを選びましょう。

Talk 1

1. Who is the speaker?

(A) A real estate agent

(B) A designer

(C) A sales clerk

(D) A banker

2. Where is the apartment?

(A) Near a beach

(B) Beside a park

(C) In a small town

(D) Close to the man's office

3. What can the woman do for the man?

(A) Send some photos

(B) Show the apartment to him

(C) Call her manager

(D) Contact a moving company

Talk 2

4. Who is Frank Thomas?

(A) A cleaner

(B) A building manager

(C) A house builder

(D) A gardener

5. What will workers do?

(A) Fix the elevator

(B) Build new balconies

(C) Replace doors

(D) Paint walls

6. What will listeners do?

(A) Use the stairs

(B) Clean their balconies

(C) Close their windows

(D) Unlock their doors

Vocabulary Builder (B)

CheckLink   DL 162   CD2-70

次の 1 ～ 8 の意味に合うものを a ～ h から選びましょう。その後で、音声を聞いて答えを確認しましょう。

1. furniture （   ）　　**2.** view （   ）　　**3.** dormitory （   ）　　**4.** garage （   ）

5. design （   ）　　**6.** cost （   ）　　**7.** provide （   ）　　**8.** convenient （   ）

a. 設計 (する)	**b.** 車庫、ガレージ	**c.** 家具	**d.** 便利な
e. 眺め	**f.** 費用 (がかかる)	**g.** 寮	**h.** 提供する

Part 5 Sentence Completion 【短文穴埋め問題】

英語の主語と動詞の使い方にはルールがあるので注意しましょう。

主語と動詞の一致

● 主語が単数か複数かで動詞の形が変わります。

単数	複数
Ken **lives** in Tokyo. The store **opens** at 10:00.	Ken and Sue **live** in Tokyo. The stores **open** at 10:00.

● everyone、every、each を使う場合、主語が複数でも動詞は単数の場合と変わりません。

単数	複数
Everyone likes Susan. **Each** table **is** new.	**Every** dog and cat **likes** Susan. **Each** table and chair **is** new.

● 主語が all、most、some、no などを伴う場合、その後の名詞が単数か複数かによって動詞の形が決まります。

単数	複数
All furniture **is** on sale. **Some** jewelry **is** very expensive.	**All** items **are** on sale. **Some** rings **are** very expensive.

● 主語と動詞の間に語句が入る場合の動詞の形に気をつけましょう。

単数	複数
The **book** on the desk **belongs** to Peter.	The **books** on the desk **belong** to Peter.

Warming Up

CheckLink

正しい選択肢を選び、文を完成させましょう。

1. Everyone (**a.** make   **b.** makes) mistakes.
2. Each student (**a.** make   **b.** makes) a short speech in English.
3. Some people (**a.** make   **b.** makes) interesting videos on YouTube.
4. The birds (**a.** make   **b.** makes) a lot of noise in the morning.

Now You Try!

CheckLink

4つの選択肢から最も適切なものを選び、文を完成させましょう。

1. The chairs in the living room ------- new.
   (A) is   (B) are   (C) has been   (D) was

2. The cost of the new window ------- $250.
   (A) are   (B) be   (C) is   (D) were

3. Most rooms in the hotel ------- Wi-Fi service.
   (A) has   (B) have   (C) is having   (D) has had

4. The house for sale ------- three bedrooms and two bathrooms.
   (A) has   (B) have   (C) having   (D) are having

5. Every room in Sun Apartments ------- an ocean view.
   (A) provide   (B) provides   (C) are providing   (D) have provided

6. A new dormitory for the students------- near the campus.
   (A) open   (B) have opened   (C) are opening   (D) has opened

7. House prices in the city ------- this year.
   (A) goes up   (B) has gone up   (C) is going up   (D) have gone up

8. This convenient neighborhood ------- popular with young couples.
   (A) become   (B) are becoming   (C) is becoming   (D) have become

Part 6　Text Completion 【長文穴埋め問題】

選択肢に語尾の異なる語句が並んでいる場合は、どの品詞が当てはまるか文を見てよく考えましょう。例えば、次のようなものがヒントになります。

- 冠詞・形容詞の後ろ ➡ 名詞 (a **car**, black **car**)
- 動詞の前後 ➡ 副詞 (**quickly** check, study **hard**)
- 副詞の後ろ ➡ 形容詞または副詞 (really **nice**, really **nicely**)

Warming Up

CheckLink

正しい選択肢を選び、文を完成させましょう。

1. The house has a nice (**a.** view　**b.** viewing).
2. Bob talks so (**a.** excited　**b.** excitedly) about his new home.
3. The moving company works (**a.** careful　**b.** carefully).
4. The apartment is in a very (**a.** quiet　**b.** quietly) neighborhood.

Now You Try!

CheckLink

4つの選択肢から最も適切なものを選び、文を完成させましょう。

Questions 1–4 refer to the following letter.

Dear Tom,

Thank you for coming to our office yesterday.　Today, I found a ------- house with
1.
two bedrooms.　The design is very -------.　The house ------- large windows.　It is 10
2.　　　　　　　　**3.**
years old.　I know you want a new house, but I think you will really like it.　-------.
4.
Please call or e-mail for more information.

Best regards,

Laura Bixby
Town and Country Real Estate

1. (A) beauty　　　(B) beautiful　　　(C) beautifully　　　(D) beautify

2. (A) interest　　　(B) interesting　　　(C) interests　　　(D) interested

3. (A) has　　　(B) is having　　　(C) had　　　(D) has had

4. (A) I sent it this morning.　　　(B) That's a good idea.
   (C) I think you will like the price, too.　　　(D) It will arrive next week.

Part 7 Reading Comprehension 【読解問題】

質問の中には、What is suggested about …?（…について何がわかりますか）や What is probably true about …?（…について正しいと考えられることは何ですか）のように、本文に答えがはっきりと述べられておらず、与えられた情報から推測する必要があるものもあります。

 Warming Up   CheckLink

次の文を読んで、答えを推測する必要のある質問に答えましょう。

> There is a large truck in front of the Andersons' house. Several people are putting tables, chairs and beds into the truck.

What is probably true about the Andersons?
（Anderson 家について正しいと考えられることは何ですか）

(A) They ordered some furniture.   (B) They live in an apartment.

(C) They work in a furniture store.   (D) They are moving.

 **Now You Try!**   CheckLink

文書を読んで、設問に対する最も適切な答えを選びましょう。

Questions 1–2 refer to the following advertisement.

YOUR DREAM HOUSE!

You have found your dream house, but do you need a home loan? Then talk to us. We have given loans to millions of families across the United States. Our team will give you advice and make a great plan for you. Make an appointment today!

CRB HOME LOANS (since 1995)
Contact us today at: crbhomeloans.com

---

1. What kind of service does the business provide?

   (A) Home loans   (B) Home security

   (C) House cleaning   (D) Family support

2. What is probably true about the company?

   (A) It has helped many people.   (B) It offers online meetings.

   (C) It is a family business.   (D) It is a small company.

Questions 3–5 refer to the following form.

QUESTIONS FOR HOME BUYERS

Name: Michael Donaldson   Date: February 2

Address: 2468 Glenworth Drive   Tel: 555-1928

Apartment 802   E-mail: mdonaldson501@inward.com

1. Number of people in your family?   (1) 2 3 4 5 6
2. Number of bedrooms?   1 (2) 3 4
3. Type of house?   ☑ New ☐ Used ☐ Not sure
4. Special requests?   a large kitchen, a two-car garage, near a fitness center
5. Price range?
   ☐ $200,000 - $300,000   ☐ $300,000 - $400,000   ☑ $400,000 - $500,000
6. Moving date?   April or May

Thank you!

3. What is suggested about Mr. Donaldson?
   (A) He has a large family.
   (B) He does not drive.
   (C) He works at home.
   (D) He exercises regularly.

4. Which house will he probably like?
   (A) A new house with three bedrooms
   (B) An old house with a large kitchen
   (C) A new two-bedroom house with a two-car garage
   (D) An old three-bedroom house near a fitness center

5. When will he probably move?
   (A) In spring
   (B) In summer
   (C) In autumn
   (D) In winter

トピック オフィス 文法 他動詞・自動詞

Vocabulary Builder A

CheckLink 🎧 DL 163 💿 CD2-71

次の1～8の意味に合うものをa～hから選びましょう。その後で、音声を聞いて答えを確認しましょう。

1. cabinet（　）　　**2.** drawer（　）　　**3.** document（　）　　**4.** shelf（　）

5. supply（　）　　**6.** co-worker（　）　　**7.** maintenance（　）　　**8.** turn on（　）

a. 同僚	**b.** 書類	**c.** 備品、供給する	**d.** 引き出し
e. （電気などを）つける	**f.** 棚	**g.** 保守点検	**h.** 戸棚、キャビネット

Part 1 Photographs 【写真描写問題】

1人の人物の動作が行われている場所や、人物と物との位置関係について、前置詞を使って表す文を学びましょう。

Warming Up

CheckLink 🎧 DL 164 💿 CD2-72

音声を聞いて空所の語句を書き取り、写真を最も適切に描写しているものを選びましょう。

(A) She's looking at the monitor ＿＿＿＿＿＿ her.

(B) She's holding the phone ＿＿＿＿＿＿ her left hand.

(C) She's standing ＿＿＿＿＿＿＿ ＿＿＿＿＿＿＿ ＿＿＿＿＿＿＿ her desk.

(D) She's writing ＿＿＿＿＿＿ a newspaper.

Now You Try!

CheckLink 🎧 DL 165 ～ 166 💿 CD2-73 ～ 💿 CD2-74

写真を描写する4つの音声を聞いて、最も適切なものを選びましょう。

1

Ⓐ Ⓑ Ⓒ Ⓓ

2

Ⓐ Ⓑ Ⓒ Ⓓ

Part 2　Question-Response 【応答問題】

Why で始まる疑問文は理由について尋ねます。一般的には答えに "Because" が使われますが、"Why are you late?" という質問に対して "I took the wrong bus." のように答えることもあります。注意して正しい理由を聞き取りましょう。

Warming Up
CheckLink　DL 167 ~ 168　CD2-75 ~ CD2-76

音声を聞いて空所の語句を書き取り、質問に対する最も適切な応答を選びましょう。

1. Why is the drawer open?

(A) Some _____.

(B) In the _____ drawer.

(C) _____ William.

2. Why is the printer making that sound?

(A) Fifty _____.

(B) It's out of _____.

(C) Because he is _____.

Now You Try!
CheckLink　DL 169 ~ 172　CD2-77 ~ CD2-80

質問とそれに対する 3 つの応答を聞いて、最も適切なものを選びましょう。

1. Ⓐ Ⓑ Ⓒ　　　**2.** Ⓐ Ⓑ Ⓒ　　　**3.** Ⓐ Ⓑ Ⓒ　　　**4.** Ⓐ Ⓑ Ⓒ

Part 3　Conversations 【会話問題】

会話の中に Yes か No で答える疑問文が登場することがあります。カギとなる情報が与えられるかもしれないので、どのように答えるか注意して聞きましょう。

Warming Up
CheckLink　DL 173 ~ 174　CD2-81 ~ CD2-82

音声を聞いて空所の語句を書き取り、質問に対する最も適切な答えを選びましょう。

> **M:** Kim, I need to ¹_____ copies for today's ²_____, but the copy machine is out of ³_____. Do we have any?
>
> **W:** Yes, it's on the bottom ⁴_____ of the ⁵_____.

1. What does the man want to do?

(A) Write a report
(B) Make some copies
(C) Draw a picture
(D) Order some supplies

2. What is the man looking for?

(A) Pens　(B) Ink　(C) A copy machine　(D) Paper

3. What will the man do next?

(A) Open a window　(B) Attend a meeting　(C) Send a file　(D) Look in a cabinet

Now You Try!

CheckLink | DL 175 ~ 178 | CD2-83 ~ CD2-86

会話を聞いて、質問に対する最も適切な答えを選びましょう。

Conversation 1

1. What is the conversation about?
- (A) A president
- (B) A singer
- (C) An actor
- (D) A co-worker

2. When will Jerry move to San Francisco?
- (A) This week
- (B) Next week
- (C) This month
- (D) Next month

3. What will the woman do?
- (A) Move to a new city
- (B) Change jobs
- (C) Call a co-worker
- (D) Plan a party

Conversation 2

4. What are the speakers talking about?
- (A) A camera
- (B) A computer
- (C) A copy machine
- (D) A printer

5. What does the man suggest?
- (A) Using a different machine
- (B) Pressing the reset button
- (C) Switching the power off and on
- (D) Reading the manual

6. What will the woman do?
- (A) Tell the office manager
- (B) Talk to the maintenance department
- (C) Call a copy machine company
- (D) Order a new machine

Part 4 Talks

【説明文問題】

理由や目的を問う質問では、答えの選択肢が To build a house のように、To の後に動詞が続くかたちになっていることがあります。この場合、動詞がキーワードになります。

Warming Up

CheckLink | DL 179 ~ 180 | CD2-87 ~ CD2-88

音声を聞いて空所の語句を書き取り、質問に対する最も適切な答えを選びましょう。

Hello, this is Barns Travel . Yesterday I four boxes of
 clips. Please ⁴_____ that to four boxes of ⁵_____ clips.
Also, could you add 10 ⁶_____ to my order? Thank you.

1. Why is the speaker calling?
- (A) To ask about the size of a product
- (B) To ask about a delivery date
- (C) To cancel a reservation
- (D) To change his order

77

2. What items will the speaker receive?

(A) Small clips　　(B) Medium clips　　(C) Large clips　　(D) Color clips

3. What other item did the speaker order?

(A) Pens　　　　(B) Erasers　　　　(C) Pencils　　　　(D) Notebooks

Now You Try!

 CheckLink DL 181 ~ 184 CD2-89 ~ CD2-92

説明文を聞いて、質問に対する最も適切な答えを選びましょう。

Talk 1

1. What is the purpose of the talk?

(A) To ask for help

(B) To meet a manager

(C) To answer a question

(D) To give information

2. What is Mark's position in the company?

(A) President

(B) Vice president

(C) Office manager

(D) Assistant office manager

3. What will happen tomorrow?

(A) There will be a meeting.

(B) The office will close.

(C) A trip will begin.

(D) A new manager will come.

Talk 2

4. What is the topic of the talk?

(A) Schedules

(B) Office space

(C) Office supplies

(D) Maintenance

5. Why did the speaker send the documents?

(A) To get feedback

(B) To buy a cabinet

(C) To look at a design

(D) To order some desks

6. Who will come on March 31?

(A) New owners

(B) Builders

(C) Moving company workers

(D) New staff

Vocabulary Builder (B)

CheckLink　　DL 185　　CD2-93

次の 1 ～ 8 の意味に合うものを a ～ h から選びましょう。その後で、音声を聞いて答えを確認しましょう。

1. department（　）　**2.** office hours（　）　**3.** set up（　）　**4.** device（　）

5. stairs（　）　**6.** require（　）　**7.** assistance（　）　**8.** cooperation（　）

a. 支援、援助	**b.** 協力	**c.** 部、部門	**d.** 設定する
e. 業務時間	**f.** 機器、装置	**g.** 必要とする	**h.** 階段

Part 5 Sentence Completion 【短文穴埋め問題】

英語の動詞は他動詞と自動詞に分けることができます。見分け方のポイントは、動詞の後ろに目的となるものが続くかどうかです。

他動詞

● 他動詞の文は〈主語＋動詞＋目的語（＝名詞または代名詞）〉という形をしています。
*Bill **likes** tennis. / The company **makes** toys. / I'll **read** the report this afternoon.*

他動詞の例（主に他動詞として使われるもの）

attend　bring　buy　call　contact　discuss　explain　get　give　have　hold
introduce　invite　join　like　make　meet　offer　order　read　rent　request　see
send　show　suggest　take　tell　visit　watch　want

自動詞

● 自動詞の文は〈主語＋動詞〉という形をしています（目的語は必要ありません）。
*Mary often **arrives** early. / It **rained** last night. / The children **are laughing**.*

自動詞の例（主に自動詞として使われるもの）

agree　appear　arrive　belong　come　dance　fall　go　happen　laugh　lie
listen　look　occur　rain　search　seem　sit　sleep　smile　stay　swim　talk
travel　wait　walk　work

● 自動詞の後ろに目的語が来る場合は前置詞を使います。
*Let's **talk** <u>about</u> our trip. / I **stayed** <u>with</u> my uncle in L.A. / He's **looking** <u>for</u> his glasses.*

Warming Up

CheckLink

次の文の動詞に線を引いて、他動詞か自動詞か選びましょう。

1. Jane always makes breakfast.　　　　（ **a.** 他動詞　 **b.** 自動詞 ）

2. Listen to your boss.　　　　（ **a.** 他動詞　 **b.** 自動詞 ）

3. Please wait for me after class.　　　　（ **a.** 他動詞　 **b.** 自動詞 ）

4. I took a taxi to school.　　　　（ **a.** 他動詞　 **b.** 自動詞 ）

Now You Try!

CheckLink

4 つの選択肢から最も適切なものを選び、文を完成させましょう。

1. Please ------- your e-mail for important announcements.
(A) check　(B) look　(C) wait　(D) work

2. Mr. Brady ------- about some plans for the office layout.
(A) saw　(B) looked　(C) made　(D) talked

3. On most days, William ------- his office at 5:00.
(A) goes　(B) leaves　(C) works　(D) stays

4. Ms. Birch will -------- the sales department next week.
(A) belong　(B) go　(C) join　(D) come

5. The Southview office is ------- for some new office equipment.
(A) looking　(B) ordering　(C) requesting　(D) suggesting

6. A computer expert from Sims Company will ------- our office.
(A) come　(B) visit　(C) arrive　(D) travel

7. Hanson Electric Company is ------- office space.
(A) looking　(B) waiting　(C) renting　(D) searching

8. Every Monday morning, the office head ------- to the staff about their work schedules.
(A) gives　(B) contacts　(C) tells　(D) talks

Part 6 Text Completion 【長文穴埋め問題】

p.16 と p.34 で学んだように、単語の終わりの形は品詞を判断するのに役立ちます。品詞がわかると、文の中でどのような働きをするのかがわかります。ここでは動詞の語尾の形を見てみましょう。

【動詞の見分け方】

cre**ate**　wid**en**　beaut**ify**　energ**ize**

Warming Up

ⓒ CheckLink

正しい選択肢を選び、文を完成させましょう。

1. The company will (**a.** shorten　**b.** short) its office hours.
2. In our office, we often (**a.** communication　**b.** communicate) by e-mail.
3. We will (**a.** finalize　**b.** finally) our new business plan next week.
4. Please (**a.** simply　**b.** simplify) your report and give it to me tomorrow.

Now You Try!

ⓒ CheckLink

4 つの選択肢から最も適切なものを選び、文を完成させましょう。

Questions 1–4 refer to the following notice.

I hope you all like our new office lunchroom. -------.
1.

＊Wash all ------- plates and cups after use.
2.
＊Put empty bottles ------- the recycling box.
3.
＊Throw away all food boxes after you eat.

Remember, the room is for everyone. Please ------- and follow the rules.
4.

Thank you.

NOTES empty 空っぽの throw away 捨てる

1. (A) Please choose your favorite layout. (B) Please close the door.
   (C) Please do not eat in the room. (D) Please follow the rules below.

2. (A) dirt　(B) dirtiness　(C) dirty　(D) dirtily

3. (A) in　(B) at　(C) for　(D) to

4. (A) cooperate　(B) cooperation　(C) cooperative　(D) cooperatively

Part **7** Reading Comprehension 【読解問題】

文書に登場するキーワードの多くが、選択肢では別の語句に言い換えられていることがあります。同じ意味を持つ表現をできるだけたくさん覚えるようにしましょう。

■ Warming Up ↻CheckLink

次の 1～8 の語句と同じ意味を持つものを a～h から選びましょう。

1. difficulty（　） **2.** require（　） **3.** document（　） **4.** response（　）

5. equipment（　） **6.** pleased（　） **7.** depart（　） **8.** colleague（　）

a. tools	**b.** co-worker	**c.** paper	**d.** answer
e. happy	**f.** problem	**g.** leave	**h.** need

■ Now You Try! ↻CheckLink

文書を読んで、設問に対する最も適切な答えを選びましょう。

Questions 1–2 refer to the following memo.

MEMO

To all office managers

How to Set Up Your Personal Printer

① Turn on the printer. The On/Off switch is on the left side.

② Put in the ink cartridges.

③ Connect the USB cable from the printer to the computer.

④ On your computer, select the **Start** button and find **Printer Settings**.

⑤ Under **Options**, select **Add a Printer**. Then follow the instructions.

---

1. What are the instructions for?

(A) Setting up a computer　　　　(B) Changing printer ink cartridges

(C) Using new software　　　　　(D) Connecting a device to a computer

2. How can the managers find the printer settings?

(A) By clicking on "Start"　　　　(B) By selecting "Options"

(C) By choosing "Add a Printer"　(D) By looking at a Web site

Questions 3–5 refer to the following notice.

Notice of Elevator Check

Friday, December 11
7:30 A.M. - 12:30 P.M.

You cannot use the elevator during this time. Please take the stairs.

- Please do not invite customers for a morning meeting on this day.
- You may take your lunch break after 12:30, instead of the regular time of 12:00 P.M.
- If you require assistance, call Nancy at 555-7109.

Steve Wilks, Office Manager

NOTE instead of … …の代わりに

3. When cannot workers use the elevator?

(A) Before 7:30 A.M.

(B) Between 12:00 P.M. and 12:30 P.M.

(C) After 12:30 P.M.

(D) All day

4. What will workers do on December 11?

(A) Telephone Steve Wilks

(B) Eat lunch at the normal time

(C) Use the stairs

(D) Have a morning meeting

5. Why will workers call Nancy?

(A) To schedule a meeting

(B) To cancel an appointment

(C) To confirm a reservation

(D) To ask for help

Employment

トピック　就職・求人　　文法　動名詞・不定詞

Vocabulary Builder (A)

CheckLink　DL 186　CD3-02

次の 1 ～ 8 の意味に合うものを a ～ h から選びましょう。その後で、音声を聞いて答えを確認しましょう。

1. résumé （　　）　　**2.** candidate （　　）　　**3.** interview （　　）　　**4.** hire （　　）

5. experience （　　）　　**6.** employee （　　）　　**7.** introduce （　　）　　**8.** paid vacation （　　）

a. 面接（する）	**b.** 雇う	**c.** 従業員	**d.** 履歴書
e. 有給休暇	**f.** 候補者	**g.** 経験	**h.** 紹介する

Part 1　Photographs

【写真描写問題】

人物同士の位置関係や、人物の動作が行われている場所について、前置詞を使って表す文を学びましょう。

Warming Up

CheckLink　DL 187　CD3-03

音声を聞いて空所の語句を書き取り、写真を最も適切に描写しているものを選びましょう。

(A) They're standing _____ _____ each other.

(B) One of the women is placing a résumé _____ the desk.

(C) They're sitting _____ _____ each other.

(D) One of the women is writing _____ a notebook.

Now You Try!

CheckLink　DL 188 ～ 189　CD3-04 ～ CD3-05

写真を描写する 4 つの音声を聞いて、最も適切なものを選びましょう。

①

Ⓐ Ⓑ Ⓒ Ⓓ

②

Ⓐ Ⓑ Ⓒ Ⓓ

Part 2 Question-Response 【応答問題】

How で始まる疑問文は、"How do you come to school?" や "How do you use this app?" のように方法を尋ねます。また、"How much" や "How big" のように、他の語句と一緒に使われることもあります。いろんなタイプの How を使った疑問文に慣れておきましょう。

Warming Up ↻CheckLink 🎧 DL 190 ~ 191 ◉CD3-06 ~ ◉CD3-07

音声を聞いて空所の語句を書き取り、質問に対する最も適切な応答を選びましょう。

1. How did you learn about our company?

   (A) _____ week.

   (B) _____ your homepage.

   (C) _____ Boston.

2. How big is your company?

   (A) It's a _____ company.

   (B) An _____ building.

   (C) We have a _____ of 200.

Now You Try! ↻CheckLink 🎧 DL 192 ~ 195 ◉CD3-08 ~ ◉CD3-11

質問とそれに対する 3 つの応答を聞いて、最も適切なものを選びましょう。

1. Ⓐ Ⓑ Ⓒ   **2.** Ⓐ Ⓑ Ⓒ   **3.** Ⓐ Ⓑ Ⓒ   **4.** Ⓐ Ⓑ Ⓒ

Part 3 Conversations 【会話問題】

就職の面接や採用など、特定のトピックに関する会話もあります。interviewやrésuméなど、キーワードとなる語句を聞き取れるように、TOEICによく出る語句をできるだけたくさん覚えましょう。

Warming Up ↻CheckLink 🎧 DL 196 ~ 197 ◉CD3-12 ~ ◉CD3-13

音声を聞いて空所の語句を書き取り、質問に対する最も適切な答えを選びましょう。

> **W:** I saw the job advertisement [1]_____ your shop last week. Are you still [2]_____?
>
> **M:** Yes, we are. Do you have any [3]_____?
>
> **W:** Yes. Here's my [4]_____. I worked in a [5]_____ in New York for five years.

1. Where did the woman see the advertisement?

   (A) In the newspaper   (B) On a Web site   (C) In a magazine   (D) Outside a store

2. What did the man ask the woman about?

   (A) Her experience   (B) Her address   (C) Her hometown   (D) Her hobby

3. Where did the woman work before?

   (A) In a bookstore   (B) In a bank   (C) In a restaurant   (D) In a shoe store

Now You Try!

CheckLink DL 198 ~ 201 CD3-14 ~ CD3-17

会話を聞いて、質問に対する最も適切な答えを選びましょう。

Conversation 1

1. What kind of meeting is it?

(A) A training session

(B) A job interview

(C) A sales meeting

(D) A staff meeting

2. What does the man ask about?

(A) Office hours

(B) Vacation days

(C) The salary

(D) The number of workers

3. What will the man receive?

(A) A letter

(B) A schedule

(C) An order

(D) A phone call

Conversation 2

4. What is the conversation about?

(A) Job candidates

(B) Supplies

(C) Staff members

(D) Customers

5. Where do the speakers work?

(A) At a computer company

(B) At a sports equipment maker

(C) At a car maker

(D) At a clothing company

6. What will the speakers do?

(A) Give Tom and Helen a factory tour

(B) Look at Helen's designs

(C) Interview another person

(D) Offer Tom a job

Part 4 Talks

【説明文問題】

トークには、日付や時刻、料金や数量に関する情報が含まれていることがあります。こうした情報を聞きながら覚えておきましょう。

Warming Up

CheckLink DL 202 ~ 203 CD3-18 ~ CD3-19

音声を聞いて空所の語句を書き取り、質問に対する最も適切な答えを選びましょう。

> Hello, Brenda. This is Chris Woods calling from Sinclair Technologies. Thank you for coming to the ¹_____ last Friday. We want you to come for a ²_____ interview for the IT ³_____. Please ⁴_____ me tomorrow between 9 A.M. and 5 P.M. Then we can arrange the day and ⁵_____ of the interview. Thank you.

1. Who is the speaker calling?

(A) A teacher   (B) A co-worker   (C) A job candidate   (D) A customer

2. What did the speaker do last Friday?

(A) He had a meeting.　　(B) He ordered some computers.

(C) He canceled an appointment.　　(D) He went on a business trip.

3. What will Brenda do tomorrow between 9 A.M. and 5 P.M.?

(A) Call Mr. Woods　　(B) Send an e-mail

(C) Check a Web site　　(D) Go to an IT fair

Now You Try!

 CheckLink　 DL 204 ~ 207　 CD3-20 ~ CD3-23

説明文を聞いて、質問に対する最も適切な答えを選びましょう。

Talk 1

1. What is the purpose of the talk?

(A) To tell the company's history

(B) To announce a job opening

(C) To talk about the company's products

(D) To welcome new employees

2. What does the speaker's company sell?

(A) Furniture

(B) Car accessories

(C) Food

(D) Clothing

3. What will the listeners do on September 1?

(A) Begin their training

(B) Have a health check-up

(C) Start working

(D) Go to a welcome party

Talk 2

4. Where is the speaker?

(A) At a birthday party

(B) At a welcome party

(C) At a wedding party

(D) At a picnic party

5. How long was Mike a sales manager?

(A) 10 years

(B) 15 years

(C) 20 years

(D) 25 years

6. What is the company's goal?

(A) Hiring more workers

(B) Moving its office

(C) Building a factory

(D) Growing the business

Vocabulary Builder B

CheckLink　DL 208　CD3-24

次の1〜8の意味に合うものをa〜hから選びましょう。その後で、音声を聞いて答えを確認しましょう。

1. retire (　)　　**2.** overtime (　)　　**3.** apply (　)　　**4.** accept (　)
5. opening (　)　　**6.** knowledge (　)　　**7.** degree (　)　　**8.** position (　)

a. 残業、時間外の、時間外に　　**b.** 職、立場　　**c.** 退職する　　**d.** 知識
e. 応募する　　**f.** 職の空き　　**g.** 学位　　**h.** 受け入れる

Part 5　Sentence Completion　【短文穴埋め問題】

動詞の後ろには動名詞や不定詞が続くことがあります。どんな動詞の後ろにどちらが続くか確認しましょう。

動名詞

● 動名詞は動詞に ing がついた形をしており、動詞と名詞の役割をします。
*Sally **enjoys traveling**. / Kenji **practices playing** the guitar.*

後ろに動名詞が続く動詞の例

avoid　consider　dislike　enjoy　finish　miss　practice　quit　recommend　suggest

不定詞

● 不定詞は〈to ＋動詞の原形〉という形をしています。
*We **hope to visit** Japan someday. / Jim **expects to pass** the test.*

後ろに不定詞が続く動詞の例

agree　decide　expect　hope　learn　need　offer　plan　promise　refuse　wait　want　would like

Warming Up

CheckLink

正しい選択肢を選び、文を完成させましょう。

1. Paul wants (**a.** singing　**b.** to sing) in a band someday.
2. Margaret dislikes (**a.** cooking　**b.** to cook).
3. Alice offered (**a.** driving　**b.** to drive) me to the station.
4. I quit (**a.** drinking　**b.** to drink) coffee at night.

Now You Try!

CheckLink

4 つの選択肢から最も適切なものを選び、文を完成させましょう。

1. We are planning ------- 20 employees next year.
   (A) hire   (B) hiring   (C) hires   (D) to hire

2. Some employees refused ------- overtime.
   (A) work   (B) worked   (C) working   (D) to work

3. Ms. Harker would like ------- the company.
   (A) join   (B) to join   (C) joins   (D) joining

4. Cathy will finish ------- candidates tomorrow.
   (A) interviews   (B) to interview   (C) interviewing   (D) interviewed

5. John Evans decided ------- and start a new business.
   (A) retired   (B) to retire   (C) retiring   (D) retires

6. The company president promised ------- everyone's salary.
   (A) raising   (B) raise   (C) to raise   (D) raised

7. The manager is considering ------- Mr. Simpson to the London office.
   (A) sending   (B) send   (C) to send   (D) sent

8. SafeFlight Air agreed ------- its employees more vacation days.
   (A) give   (B) giving   (C) to give   (D) gave

Part 6 Text Completion 【長文穴埋め問題】

選択肢に同じ品詞が並んでいて、すべて空所に当てはまりそうな場合は、その前の文を見て、どの語句が文脈に合うか考えましょう。

Warming Up ↻CheckLink

正しい選択肢を選び、文を完成させましょう。

1. Mick's Café is looking for waiters. No (**a.** experience   **b.** reservation) is necessary.

2. The office manager introduced Helen to everyone. She enjoyed meeting her new (**a.** classmates   **b.** co-workers).

3. The company has decided to invite six candidates for a job interview. I will (**a.** contact   **b.** order) them this afternoon.

4. Everyone will enjoy George's retirement speech. His speeches are always (**a.** sad   **b.** funny).

Now You Try! ↻CheckLink

4 つの選択肢から最も適切なものを選び、文を完成させましょう。

Questions 1–4 refer to the following letter.

Dear Ms. Paine,

I saw the opening for a full-time English teacher on your Web site. -------. I have
1.
a teaching -------. I also have 10 years of experience, and I am a very hard -------.
2.   **3.**
I hope to talk about the ------- with you soon.
4.

Sincerely yours,

Bruce Warner

1. (A) I would like to apply for the job.   (B) I have a Web site, too.
   (C) I accept your kind offer.   (D) I am looking for a part-time position.

2. (A) assistant   (B) license   (C) schedule   (D) staff

3. (A) work   (B) working   (C) works   (D) worker

4. (A) position   (B) loan   (C) school   (D) research

Part 7 Reading Comprehension 【読解問題】

Part 7では、文書の中で述べられていない情報が問われることがあります。そのような場合は4つの選択肢のうち述べられているものを3つ見つけましょう。残ったものが答えです。

 ## Warming Up

CheckLink

次の求人広告の一部を読んで、質問に答えましょう。

> Candidates must have a degree in journalism and two years of experience. Candidates must also have excellent communication, presentation and reporting skills.

What is NOT a requirement for the position?（その職の必要条件でないものは何ですか）

(A) A degree
(B) Experience
(C) Communication skills
(D) Research skills

NOTE requirement 必要条件

 ## Now You Try!

CheckLink

文書を読んで、設問に対する最も適切な答えを選びましょう。

Questions 1–3 refer to the following advertisement.

> ### JOB OPENING
>
> **Crestler Motors** is looking for an assistant in the customer service department. Candidates must have customer service experience, basic computer knowledge and a university degree. Candidates also need good communication skills. Please apply by January 31. Interviews will take place between March 3 and 7. For more information, visit us at www.crestlermotors.com.

1. What position is available?

(A) Driver (B) Engineer (C) Sales Manager (D) Customer service assistant

2. What is NOT a requirement for the position?

(A) Experience
(B) A basic knowledge of cars
(C) A university education
(D) Communication skills

3. What will Crestler Motors do between March 3 and 7?

(A) Hire a new manager
(B) Open a new customer service office
(C) Interview candidates
(D) Train new workers

Questions 4–6 refer to the following e-mail.

From:	Victor Sanders
To:	Anne Daly
Subject:	Your interview
Date:	May 10

Dear Ms. Daly,

Thank you for coming to the interview for the marketing manager position. We have finished our interviews, and have decided to offer you the job.

Will you accept the position? Please give me your answer by May 15. I'm looking forward to hearing from you soon.

Sincerely,

Victor Sanders

4. What is the purpose of the e-mail?
   (A) To change Ms. Daly's appointment
   (B) To offer Ms. Daly a job
   (C) To invite Ms. Daly for an interview
   (D) To answer Ms. Daly's question

5. What job did Ms. Daly apply for?
   (A) Marketing manager
   (B) Sales assistant
   (C) IT specialist
   (D) Travel agent

6. What will Ms. Daly do by May 15?
   (A) Start a job
   (B) Meet with the company president
   (C) Make a decision
   (D) Move to a new city

Meetings

トピック 会議・打ち合わせ 　文 法 現在分詞・過去分詞

Vocabulary Builder (A)

CheckLink 　DL 209 　CD3-25

次の 1 ～ 8 の意味に合うものを a ～ h から選びましょう。その後で、音声を聞いて答えを確認しましょう。

1. attend (　　) 　**2.** absent (　　) 　**3.** reschedule (　　) 　**4.** meeting (　　)
5. on schedule (　　) 　**6.** behind (　　) 　**7.** correct (　　) 　**8.** business trip (　　)

a. 会議、打ち合わせ	**b.** 訂正する、正しい	**c.** 参加する、出席する	**d.** 予定通りに
e. 予定を変更する	**f.** 遅れて、後ろに	**g.** 欠席して	**h.** 出張

Part 1 　Photographs

【写真描写問題】

3 人以上の人物が写っている場合、1 人の人物について述べられているのか、複数の人物について述べられているのか、位置関係にも注意して聞きましょう。

Warming Up

CheckLink 　DL 210 　CD3-26

音声を聞いて空所の語句を書き取り、写真を最も適切に描写しているものを選びましょう。

(A) They're _____ lunch together.
(B) One of the women is _____ glasses.
(C) The man is _____ a letter.
(D) One of the women is _____ behind the man.

Now You Try!

CheckLink 　DL 211 ～ 212 　CD3-27 ～ CD3-28

写真を描写する 4 つの音声を聞いて、最も適切なものを選びましょう。

❶

Ⓐ Ⓑ Ⓒ Ⓓ

❷

Ⓐ Ⓑ Ⓒ Ⓓ

Part 2　Question-Response　【応答問題】

付加疑問文は「…ですよね？」と確認をする疑問文で、"This book is yours, **isn't it**?" や "Tom doesn't live in Tokyo, **does he**?" のように、文の最後にことばを付け加えて作ります。答え方は Yes か No で答える疑問文と同じです。

Warming Up　⟲CheckLink　🎧 DL 213 ~ 214　◉ CD3-29 ~ ◉ CD3-30

音声を聞いて空所の語句を書き取り、質問に対する最も適切な応答を選びましょう。

1. The project is on schedule, isn't it?

　(A) No, we're a ＿＿＿＿＿ behind.

　(B) I have the ＿＿＿＿＿.

　(C) No, in five ＿＿＿＿＿.

2. We don't have a meeting today, do we?

　(A) Yes, ＿＿＿＿＿ to meet you.

　(B) No, about ten ＿＿＿＿＿.

　(C) No, we ＿＿＿＿＿.

Now You Try!　⟲CheckLink　🎧 DL 215 ~ 218　◉ CD3-31 ~ ◉ CD3-34

質問とそれに対する3つの応答を聞いて、最も適切なものを選びましょう。

1. Ⓐ Ⓑ Ⓒ　　**2.** Ⓐ Ⓑ Ⓒ　　**3.** Ⓐ Ⓑ Ⓒ　　**4.** Ⓐ Ⓑ Ⓒ

Part 3　Conversations　【会話問題】

相手の発言に対して、"Oh, really?" や "That's too bad." のように反応を表すことがあります。反応を説明する文が続くことが多いので、注意して聞きましょう。

Warming Up　⟲CheckLink　🎧 DL 219 ~ 220　◉ CD3-35 ~ ◉ CD3-36

音声を聞いて空所の語句を書き取り、質問に対する最も適切な答えを選びましょう。

> **M:** Karen, this is the [1]＿＿＿＿＿ for today's meeting. Shall I make 20 copies?
>
> **W:** Yes, please. … No, wait! The [2]＿＿＿＿＿ team won't be here today, so we'll only need 15. Also, Bob isn't [3]＿＿＿＿＿ for his presentation. He [4]＿＿＿＿＿ more time.
>
> **M:** OK, I'll [5]＿＿＿＿＿ the schedule and then make copies.

1. What does the man show?

　(A) A sales report　　(B) A business plan　　(C) A schedule　　(D) Copy paper

2. Which team will be absent from the meeting?

　(A) The IT team　　(B) The marketing team

　(C) The sales team　　(D) The maintenance team

3. What will the man do next?

(A) Input data   (B) Make a call   (C) Change a schedule   (D) Make copies

Now You Try!

CheckLink   DL 221 ~ 224   CD3-37 ~ CD3-40

会話を聞いて、質問に対する最も適切な答えを選びましょう。

Conversation 1

1. What are the speakers talking about?

(A) A business lunch

(B) A meeting

(C) A party

(D) A seminar

2. What was Brad going to talk about?

(A) An airplane

(B) A new plan

(C) A business trip

(D) A new manager

3. Why did they cancel Brad's flight?

(A) The weather was bad.

(B) There was an accident.

(C) His airplane had engine trouble.

(D) There was a mistake.

Conversation 2

4. What did the man do this morning?

(A) He missed a train.

(B) He was late for a meeting.

(C) He met a new staff member.

(D) He did not attend a meeting.

5. What will the company do?

(A) Close an office

(B) Hire some workers

(C) Move to a new place

(D) Reschedule a meeting

6. What will the speakers receive?

(A) A new office plan

(B) A special bonus

(C) A report

(D) A mailing list

Part 4   Talks   【説明文問題】

話し手は何らかの変更について述べることがあります。どのような変更が行われるのか注意して聞きましょう。

Warming Up

CheckLink   DL 225 ~ 226   CD3-41 ~ CD3-42

音声を聞いて空所の語句を書き取り、質問に対する最も適切な答えを選びましょう。

Hi, Ann. I'm sorry, but I can't ¹_____ our ²_____ meeting. My flight is delayed because of an ³_____ problem. I won't arrive in Seattle until ⁴_____. Can we ⁵_____ the meeting for tomorrow at the ⁶_____ time?

1. What is the cause of the flight delay?

(A) Strong wind   (B) A computer problem   (C) Engine trouble   (D) Heavy snow

2. When will the speaker arrive in Seattle?

(A) This afternoon

(B) Later tonight

(C) Tomorrow morning

(D) Tomorrow afternoon

3. What is the speaker suggesting?

(A) Having an online meeting

(B) Waiting for him

(C) Meeting in a different place

(D) Rescheduling the meeting

Now You Try!

CheckLink  DL 227 ~ 230 CD3-43 ~ CD3-46

説明文を聞いて、質問に対する最も適切な答えを選びましょう。

Talk 1

1. What will the company repair?

(A) A parking lot

(B) A road

(C) A machine

(D) A sports park

2. Where will listeners park?

(A) On the street

(B) In the parking lot of a mall

(C) In the parking lot of a sports ground

(D) In another company's parking lot

3. What will listeners find in an e-mail?

(A) A telephone number

(B) A map

(C) A form

(D) A schedule

Talk 2

4. What has the city changed?

(A) The name of a street

(B) The number of buses

(C) The price of train tickets

(D) The route of a bus

5. What will the company offer?

(A) Meal coupons

(B) A shuttle service

(C) Free tickets

(D) A discount

6. What will listeners do after the meeting?

(A) Write a report

(B) Pay some money

(C) Show a card

(D) Give some information

Vocabulary Builder (B)

CheckLink　DL 231　CD3-47

次の1～8の意味に合うものをa～hから選びましょう。その後で、音声を聞いて答えを確認しましょう。

1. propose（　）　**2.** improve（　）　**3.** explain（　）　**4.** discuss（　）

5. postpone（　）　**6.** agree（　）　**7.** project（　）　**8.** policy（　）

a. 提案する　　**b.** 説明する　　**c.** 話し合う　　**d.** 賛成する
e. 計画　　**f.** 延期する　　**g.** 方針　　**h.** 改善する

Part 5 Sentence Completion 【短文穴埋め問題】

動詞の ing 形や過去分詞はいつも動詞として使われるわけではないので注意しましょう。

現在分詞

● working、writing、eating など、現在分詞は動詞に ing がついた形をしています。以下のように名詞の前や後ろに置いて形容詞のように使われることがあります。

名詞の前①：人や物がすることを表します。
　*a **training** coach / a **washing** machine / a **flying** car*

名詞の前②：ある特定の時に人や物がしていることを表します。
　*a **crying** baby / **laughing** children / **falling** leaves*

名詞の後：フレーズの一部として使われます。
　*the man **wearing** glasses (X the wearing glasses man)*
　*students **studying** in the library (X studying in the library students)*

過去分詞

● worked、written、eaten など、過去分詞の形は様々です。現在分詞と同じく、以下のように名詞の前や後ろに置いて形容詞のように使われることがあります。

名詞の前：人や物の状態を表します。
　*a **lost** child / a **used** computer / a **broken** window*

名詞の後：フレーズの一部として使われます。
　*the car **parked** across the street (X the across the street parked car)*
　*a class **taught** by Mr. Brown (X a taught by Mr. Brown class)*

Warming Up

CheckLink

日本語の意味に合うように、正しい選択肢を選びましょう。

1. すりつぶされたジャガイモ：(**a.** mashing   **b.** mashed) potatoes
2. 眠っている赤ちゃん：a (**a.** sleeping   **b.** slept) baby
3. 公園をジョギングしている人たち：the people (**a.** jogging   **b.** jogged) in the park
4. 英語で書かれた本：a book (**a.** writing   **b.** written) in English

Now You Try!

CheckLink

4 つの選択肢から最も適切なものを選び、文を完成させましょう。

1. Mr. Jones will introduce a new ------- machine at the meeting.
   (A) cleanliness   (B) cleaning   (C) cleaned   (D) cleans

2. Ms. Becker will e-mail a ------- report of yesterday's meeting.
   (A) write   (B) writing   (C) written   (D) wrote

3. The meeting -------- at 4:00 is in Room A.
   (A) starts   (B) starting   (C) started   (D) start

4. Please read the memo ------- for the next meeting.
   (A) prepares   (B) preparing   (C) prepare   (D) prepared

5. This is a list of members ------- today's meeting.
   (A) attending   (B) attend   (C) attended   (D) attends

6. The manager has received an e-mail ------- about our new project.
   (A) ask   (B) asked   (C) asking   (D) asks

7. At today's meeting, we will discuss the plan -------- by the project manager.
   (A) proposing   (B) proposes   (C) propose   (D) proposed

8. Today we will talk about the ------- changes to our company policy.
   (A) suggested   (B) suggest   (C) suggesting   (D) suggests

Part 6 Text Completion 【長文穴埋め問題】

選択肢に同じ品詞が並んでいて、すべて空所に当てはまりそうで前の文を見ても手がかりが見つからない場合は、後ろの文を見てみましょう。

Warming Up CheckLink

正しい選択肢を選び、文を完成させましょう。

1. The manager sent everyone a (**a.** package   **b.** memo) this morning. It told us the time of our afternoon meeting.
2. We need to (**a.** advertise   **b.** improve) our delivery system. I will explain the problems at the meeting.
3. The meeting room is not (**a.** available   **b.** busy) this morning. It will be free this afternoon.
4. The team (**a.** never   **b.** regularly) discusses their project. They get together every Monday morning.

Now You Try! CheckLink

4 つの選択肢から最も適切なものを選び、文を完成させましょう。

Questions 1–4 refer to the following letter.

Dear Mr. Sanders,

Today, my team and I had a meeting about your company's new Web site. We will ------- making it soon. It's going smoothly, but we still need to do several more things.
   1.

   (1) Make a final ------- on the number of pages.
         2.
   (2) Make a few changes to the -------.
              3.
   (3) Choose a few more photos and illustrations.

We will meet again on Friday. -------.
         4.

Regards,
Mike Gillis

1. (A) avoid (B) consider (C) finish (D) start
2. (A) decide (B) decision (C) deciding (D) decided
3. (A) design (B) designers (C) designing (D) designed
4. (A) Please read it. (B) There are three sizes.
   (C) Our products are very good. (D) I'll write to you again after the meeting.

99

Part 7 · Reading Comprehension 【読解問題】

Part 7 で出題される「チャット形式」の文書の設問の１つに、
  At（時間）, what does（名前）mean when he/she writes, "（文）"?
というタイプのものがあります。チャットの流れから文の意味を正確に読み取りましょう。

Warming Up

CheckLink

次の文を読んで、質問に答えましょう。

> **Bob Stone (2:48 P.M.):**   Do you want to have dinner at an Italian restaurant?
> **Lana Hanes (2: 50 P.M.):** Well, I had Italian food last night.

At 2:50 P.M., what does Ms. Hanes mean when she writes, "Well, I had Italian food last night"?（午後２時50分に、Hanesさんは "Well, I had Italian food last night" という発言で、何を意味していますか）

　(A) She wants to have Italian food.

　(B) She wants to eat dinner at home.

　(C) She does not like Italian food.

　(D) She does not want to go to an Italian restaurant.

Now You Try!

CheckLink

文書を読んで、設問に対する最も適切な答えを選びましょう。

Questions 1–3 refer to the following text-message chain.

Carl Yates (1:17 P.M.)	I couldn't reserve a meeting room. I suggest discussing our project at Robin's Café.
Wendy Andrews (1:18 P.M.)	That sounds good. Andy?
Andy Dickenson (1:19 P.M.)	That's a good idea. But I recommend Peyton's Place. It's not crowded like Robin's.
Wendy Andrews (1:20 P.M.)	Good point. And the tables are quite large. We can put our sample sketches on one.
Carl Yates (1:21 P.M.)	OK, we'll go to Peyton's Place. Let's leave the office at 3:30.
Andy Dickenson (1:22 P.M.)	Perfect!
Wendy Andrews (1:23 P.M.)	OK, see you then.

1. Why will they have a meeting outside the office?

    (A) The office is closed.   (B) It is very hot in the office.

    (C) It is convenient.   (D) The meeting rooms are not available.

2. At 1:18 P.M., what does Ms. Andrews mean when she writes, "That sounds good"?

    (A) She agrees to meet outside the office.

    (B) She is working in the office.

    (C) She often goes to Robin's Café.

    (D) She is a member of the project team.

3. What is suggested about Peyton's Place?

    (A) It is expensive.   (B) It has many tables.

    (C) It has big tables.   (D) It is near the office.

Questions 4-6 refer to the following e-mail.

To:	All staff members
From:	Thomas Bamford, General Manager
Date:	June 23
Subject:	Today's office schedule

The office will close at 3:00 today. There will be heavy snow and strong winds later this afternoon. We hope that everyone will be able to return home safely. Our regular 3:00 meeting will start at 1:45 this afternoon. We will discuss the first three items on the agenda. Other items can wait until next week.

—Thomas—

NOTE agenda 議題

4. Why will the office close early?

    (A) There was an accident.   (B) Workers will attend a party.

    (C) Bad weather is coming.   (D) There will be maintenance.

5. What will workers do at 1:45?

    (A) Attend a meeting   (B) Write a report   (C) Check their e-mail   (D) Go home

6. What is true about the office meeting?

    (A) It usually ends at 3:00.   (B) It will cover all items.

    (C) It will cover three items.   (D) It will be in a different room.

Unit 11 Clients

トピック	顧客・取引先	文法	時を表す前置詞

Vocabulary Builder A

CheckLink　DL 232　CD3-48

次の 1 ～ 8 の意味に合うものを a ～ h から選びましょう。その後で、音声を聞いて答えを確認しましょう。

1. client（　　）　　**2.** contract（　　）　　**3.** contact（　　）　　**4.** deliver（　　）

5. order form（　　）　**6.** promote（　　）　　**7.** in cash（　　）　　**8.** sign（　　）

a. 契約（書）	**b.** 顧客	**c.** 注文用紙、注文書	**d.** 現金で
e. 連絡（する）	**f.** 配達する	**g.** 促進する、宣伝する	**h.** 署名する

Part 1　Photographs

【写真描写問題】

人物の写っていない写真では、音声が流れる前に素早く写真に目を通して、写っているものに注目しましょう。また、物の位置を表す文が聞こえることを予測して待ちましょう。

Warming Up

CheckLink　DL 233　CD3-49

音声を聞いて空所の語句を書き取り、写真を最も適切に描写しているものを選びましょう。

(A) Some documents are ＿＿＿＿ ＿＿＿＿ ＿＿＿＿.

(B) A spoon is ＿＿＿＿ ＿＿＿＿ ＿＿＿＿.

(C) A pencil is ＿＿＿＿ ＿＿＿＿ ＿＿＿＿.

(D) Some coffee is ＿＿＿＿ ＿＿＿＿ ＿＿＿＿.

Now You Try!

CheckLink　DL 234 ～ 235　CD3-50 ～ CD3-51

写真を描写する 4 つの音声を聞いて、最も適切なものを選びましょう。

❶

Ⓐ Ⓑ Ⓒ Ⓓ

❷

Ⓐ Ⓑ Ⓒ Ⓓ

102

Part 2 Question-Response 【応答問題】

否定疑問文は Unit 10 で学んだ付加疑問文と同じように、「…ではないですか?」と確認するときに使います。答え方は Yes か No で答える疑問文と同じで、"Aren't we late?" という否定疑問文は "Are we late?" と同じように考えます。

Warming Up CheckLink DL 236 ~ 237 CD3-52 ~ CD3-53

音声を聞いて空所の語句を書き取り、質問に対する最も適切な応答を選びましょう。

1. Don't customers need fast delivery?
   (A) Yes, many customers _____ so.
   (B) _____ days.
   (C) In the _____.

2. Aren't you meeting your client today?
   (A) On the _____.
   (B) That's a good _____.
   (C) Yes, this _____.

Now You Try! CheckLink DL 238 ~ 241 CD3-54 ~ CD3-57

質問とそれに対する 3 つの応答を聞いて、最も適切なものを選びましょう。

1. (A) (B) (C)   2. (A) (B) (C)   3. (A) (B) (C)   4. (A) (B) (C)

Part 3 Conversations 【会話問題】

Part 3 では、"What does the man mean when he says …?" のように、会話に登場する文に対する理解を確かめる質問が出題されます。会話の状況をよく考えて答えましょう。

Warming Up CheckLink DL 242 ~ 243 CD3-58 ~ CD3-59

音声を聞いて空所の語句を書き取り、質問に対する最も適切な答えを選びましょう。

M: I'm calling about your new [1]_____ machine. You bought it one month ago. Have you had any [2]_____?

W: No, it's [3]_____ beautifully. And it's really [4]_____.

M: That's great. Just give me a call if you need any [5]_____.

---

1. What did the woman buy?
   (A) A copy machine
   (B) A cooking machine
   (C) A washing machine
   (D) A training machine

2. Why does the woman like the machine?
   (A) It is fast.   (B) It is small.   (C) It is quiet.   (D) It is light.

3. What does the man mean when he says, "That's great"?
   (A) He could talk with the woman.
   (B) He does not have any problems.
   (C) He is happy with the woman's answer.
   (D) He has the same product.

103

Now You Try!

CheckLink　DL 244 ~ 247　CD3-60 ~ CD3-63

会話を聞いて、質問に対する最も適切な答えを選びましょう。

Conversation 1

1. Who is the woman?
- (A) A truck driver
- (B) A store manager
- (C) A customer service agent
- (D) A salesperson

2. What does the man mean when he says, "It's already after three o'clock"?
- (A) He wants to change an appointment.
- (B) He is unhappy with the service.
- (C) He is going to be late.
- (D) He needs more time.

3. What will the woman do next?
- (A) Check an order form
- (B) Reorder some tables
- (C) Call her boss
- (D) Contact the driver

Conversation 2

Item	Quantity
Caps	6
Socks	8
Baseballs	10
Bats	12

4. Why is the woman calling?
- (A) To confirm an order
- (B) To request payment
- (C) To promote a sale
- (D) To announce a price change

5. Look at the graphic. What item are the speakers discussing?
- (A) Caps
- (B) Socks
- (C) Baseballs
- (D) Bats

6. When will the man receive the items?
- (A) Today
- (B) Tomorrow
- (C) In two days
- (D) In one week

Part 4　Talks

【説明文問題】

Part 4 では話し手がどこで働いているかを尋ねる問題がよく出ます。いつもはっきりと答えが述べられるわけではないので、場所を特定するキーワードを聞き取る必要があります。

Warming Up

CheckLink　DL 248 ~ 249　CD3-64 ~ CD3-65

音声を聞いて空所の語句を書き取り、質問に対する最も適切な答えを選びましょう。

> Mrs. Simpson, this is Laura Warner from Bright Spots. I'm calling about special
> ^{1}_____ on our ^{2}_____ care products. They are ^{3}_____ % off this
> ^{4}_____. Shop between 9 A.M. and 12 P.M., and you will ^{5}_____ a free
> ^{6}_____. We hope to see you soon.

1. Where does the woman work?

(A) At a fitness center   (B) At a cosmetics shop

(C) At a hospital   (D) At a sporting goods store

2. How long is the sale?

(A) Five days   (B) Ten days   (C) Two weeks   (D) One month

3. How can Mrs. Simpson receive a free gift?

(A) By paying in cash   (B) By showing her member's card

(C) By shopping online   (D) By shopping in the morning

Now You Try!   CheckLink    DL 250 ~ 253   CD3-66 ~ CD3-69

説明文を聞いて、質問に対する最も適切な答えを選びましょう。

Talk 1

1. Where does the speaker work?

(A) At a flower shop

(B) At a telephone company

(C) At a drugstore

(D) At an office supply company

2. Why is the speaker calling?

(A) To promote a product

(B) To schedule a meeting

(C) To offer after-sales service

(D) To discuss a payment

3. What will the speaker do?

(A) Call again later

(B) Add $10 to this month's bill

(C) Send some money

(D) Talk to her boss

Talk 2

4. Why is the speaker excited?

(A) A sale will start soon.

(B) Everyone will receive a bonus.

(C) He joined the company.

(D) The company has a new client.

5. Where does the speaker work?

(A) At a cleaning company

(B) At a clothing company

(C) At a Web page design company

(D) At a newspaper company

6. What will listeners receive after the meeting?

(A) A contract

(B) Some information

(C) A manual

(D) Some samples

Vocabulary Builder Ⓑ

 CheckLink　🎧 DL 254　◎ CD3-70

次の 1 ～ 8 の意味に合うものを a ～ h から選びましょう。その後で、音声を聞いて答えを確認しましょう。

1. increase（　）　**2.** continue（　）　**3.** relationship（　）　**4.** fill in（　）

5. apologize（　）　**6.** missing（　）　**7.** safety（　）　**8.** negotiate（　）

a. 交渉する	**b.** 関係	**c.** 続く、続ける	**d.** 安全
e. 謝罪する	**f.** 記入する	**g.** 増加（する）	**h.** 見つからない

Part ⑤ Sentence Completion 【短文穴埋め問題】

時を表す前置詞は、出来事がいつ起きたかを示す場合に重要なものです。時を表す前置詞を含むフレーズを見て、どのように使うのかを覚えましょう。

時を表す前置詞

● 時を表す前置詞の後ろには名詞または名詞句が続きます。

in「…に」 （月・季節・年・1日の時間帯）	*Bob went to Japan **in** June.* *Garden shops are always busy **in** spring.* *The company opened a new office **in** 2022.* *The meeting will be **in** the afternoon.*
on「…に」（曜日や特定の日）	*The sale begins **on** Monday.* *The concert is **on** New Year's Eve.*
at「…に」（時刻）	*The seminar starts **at** 10 A.M.* *The restaurant opens **at** noon.*
for「…の間」（期間）	*Sandra has worked here **for** 10 years.* *Let's take a break **for** a few minutes.*
since「…から」	*The company has been in business **since** 1953.*
from ... to ~「…から~まで」	*The store is open **from** 10 A.M. **to** 8 P.M.* *Ted lived in Seattle **from** 2010 **to** 2016.*
before「…の前に」 **during**「…の間に」 **after**「…の後に」	*Tim studied **before** dinner.* *We met interesting people **during** our trip.* *I'll call you **after** the meeting.*
by「…まで」（期限） **until**「…まで」（ある時まで続く状態）	*Please give me your report **by** Friday.* *The sale continues **until** January 31.*

Warming Up

CheckLink

正しい選択肢を選び、文を完成させましょう。

1. The class starts (**a.** at **b.** in) 2 o'clock.
2. The festival is (**a.** on **b.** in) July 1.
3. Let's have lunch (**a.** before **b.** since) the game.
4. Greg lived in Japan (**a.** for **b.** during) three years.

Now You Try!

CheckLink

4つの選択肢から最も適切なものを選び、文を完成させましょう。

1. Mr. Watson will prepare the contract ------- Friday.
   (A) at   (B) by   (C) during   (D) until

2. Renova Sports has served customers ------- 1980.
   (A) at   (B) for   (C) to   (D) since

3. Our customer service center is open ------- 10 A.M. to 6 P.M.
   (A) by   (B) at   (C) from   (D) since

4. WMC Computers delivered our order -------- noon.
   (A) since   (B) until   (C) for   (D) at

5. ------- her business trip, Ms. Jones will visit several customers.
   (A) At   (B) By   (C) During   (D) In

6. The sales manager spoke with the customer ------- two hours.
   (A) for   (B) in   (C) on   (D) until

7. We negotiated with A&H Building company -------- 11 P.M.
   (A) until   (B) during   (C) for   (D) by

8. The contract between Rev Motors and Shaw Glass Company ends ------- March 31.
   (A) at   (B) for   (C) in   (D) on

Part **6**　Text Completion　　　　　【長文穴埋め問題】

「動詞＋前置詞」「動詞＋副詞」「動詞＋副詞＋前置詞」でできているもののことを「句動詞」といいます。英語では非常に一般的に使われるので、できるだけたくさん覚えましょう。

call off（中止する）/ come up with（思い付く）/ deal with（対処する）/ fill out（記入する）/
find out（わかる）/ give away（無料で与える）/ hand out（配布する）/ keep up with（追いつく）/
look forward to（楽しみにする）/ run out of（不足する）/ sign up for（申し込む）/
take care of（処理する）/ take place（行われる）/ be in charge of（担当する）

▶ Warming Up　　　　　　　　　　　　　　　⟳ CheckLink

正しい選択肢を選び、文を完成させましょう。

1. Janet will deal (**a.** for　**b.** with) the client's questions.

2. Our client called (**a.** on　**b.** off) the meeting.

3. Bill will take care (**a.** with　**b.** of) our customers in New York.

4. Many customers have signed up (**a.** for　**b.** with) our newsletter.

▶ Now You Try!　　　　　　　　　　　　　　⟳ CheckLink

4 つの選択肢から最も適切なものを選び、文を完成させましょう。

Questions 1–4 refer to the following letter.

Dear Ms. Varner,

My name is Blake Edwards. I'm in charge ------- the customer service department
　　　　　　　　　　　　　　　　　　　　　1.
at Rex Company. Thank you very much for using our products.

Our prices will increase a little from April 1. The cost of your ------- order will go up
　　　　　　　　　　　　　　　　　　　　　　　　　　　　　　　　2.
from $900 to $918. -------. We look forward ------- continuing our relationship.
　　　　　　　　　　　　3.　　　　　　　　　　4.

Sincerely yours,

Blake Edwards

---

1. (A) at　　　　　　　(B) for　　　　　　　(C) of　　　　　　　(D) with

2. (A) regulate　　　　(B) regulation　　　　(C) regularly　　　　(D) regular

3. (A) Thank you for your order.　　　　　(B) That's a discount of 2%.
    (C) We apologize for this.　　　　　　　(D) It's a very good product.

4. (A) for　　　　　　　(B) in　　　　　　　(C) to　　　　　　　(D) with

108

Part 7 Reading Comprehension 【読解問題】

文書の中のある単語に最も近い意味を持つ選択肢を選ぶ問題が出題されることがあります。その単語が使われている文や前後の文の意味をよく考えて、ヒントを見つけましょう。

Warming Up CheckLink

次の文を読んで、質問に答えましょう。

> We received an inquiry from one of our customers. He wants to know the size and weight of our air conditioners.

The word "inquiry" in line 1, is closest in meaning to
(1 行目にある "inquiry" に最も意味が近いのは)

(A) payment   (B) order   (C) question   (D) sample

Now You Try! CheckLink

文書を読んで、設問に対する最も適切な答えを選びましょう。

Questions 1–3 refer to the following form.

Thank you for buying a Delana exercise bicycle!

Please fill in this form and send it back to us. We will only use the information in case of a safety problem with the product. Your product number is: **DWM47235**

Do you want information about new products?   Yes ☐   No ☑

Name: Kimberly Smithers

Address: 611 Danview Road, Philadelphia, Pennsylvania 49017

E-mail: kimbers72985@palmail.ad

Send to: Delana Company, 1812 Canary St., Chicago, Illinois 60018

NOTE in case of ... …の場合に

1. What does the company make?
(A) Tires   (B) Fitness equipment   (C) Safety products   (D) Toys

2. What is true about Ms. Smithers?

(A) She lives in Chicago.

(B) She bought a new television.

(C) She works for Delana Company.

(D) She does not want to receive advertisements.

3. Why will the company contact Ms. Smithers?

(A) To make an appointment

(B) To send a catalog

(C) To report trouble

(D) To request feedback

Questions 4–6 refer to the following e-mail.

To:	Roger Cook
From:	Stephanie Powell
Date:	April 30
Subject:	Payment request

Dear Mr. Cook,

I am writing about an e-mail from you on April 29. You requested a payment of $1,250 for my order of four chairs. I received them on April 11. However, one of the chairs was broken. I spoke with Mr. Tate in your customer service department on April 15. He promised to send a new chair. I will make the payment after it arrives.

Sincerely yours,

Stephanie Powell

4. Why did Ms. Powell write the e-mail?

(A) To ask for payment

(B) To apologize for a mistake

(C) To order some chairs

(D) To explain a problem

5. The word "requested" in paragraph 1, line 1, is closest in meaning to

(A) asked for   (B) made   (C) looked for   (D) received

6. What is suggested about the order?

(A) Ms. Powell received it on April 29.

(B) There was a broken item.

(C) It had the wrong items.

(D) An item was missing.

トピック　**オフィス**　　文法　**接続詞**

Vocabulary Builder Ⓐ

⟳CheckLink　🎧DL 255　◉CD3-71

次の1～8の意味に合うものをa～hから選びましょう。その後で、音声を聞いて答えを確認しましょう。

1. deadline （　　）　　**2.** security （　　）　　**3.** ID card （　　）　　**4.** branch （　　）
5. laptop （　　）　　**6.** install （　　）　　**7.** enter （　　）　　**8.** motivation （　　）

a. 安全	**b.** やる気、動機	**c.** 設置する	**d.** 締め切り、期限
e. 身分証明書	**f.** 入る	**g.** 支店、支社	**h.** ノートパソコン

Part **1** Photographs 【写真描写問題】

写真に写っていない物について述べている文は無視して、実際に写っている物について述べている文に集中しましょう。

Warming Up

⟳CheckLink　🎧DL 256　◉CD3-72

音声を聞いて空所の語句を書き取り、写真を最も適切に描写しているものを選びましょう。

(A) Chairs are _____ _____ _____.
(B) There is a camera _____ _____ _____.
(C) Boxes are _____ _____ _____.
(D) A suitcase is _____ _____ _____.

Now You Try!

⟳CheckLink　🎧DL 257～258　◉CD3-73～◉CD3-74

写真を描写する4つの音声を聞いて、最も適切なものを選びましょう。

❶

Ⓐ Ⓑ Ⓒ Ⓓ

❷

Ⓐ Ⓑ Ⓒ Ⓓ

Part 2 Question-Response 【応答問題】

選択疑問文は "Do you want coffee or tea?" のように、2 つかそれ以上の選択肢を与えて「A か B か」と尋ねる疑問文です。最後の選択肢の前には or が付きます。Yes や No では答えられないので注意しましょう。

Warming Up   CheckLink   DL 259 ~ 260   CD3-75 ~ CD3-76

音声を聞いて空所の語句を書き取り、質問に対する最も適切な応答を選びましょう。

1. Do you work alone or in a group?
   (A) Yes, I like _____.
   (B) It doesn't _____.
   (C) Usually _____.

2. Does the manager want our report on Monday or Tuesday?
   (A) _____ is Monday.
   (B) I'll _____ it on Tuesday.
   (C) Tuesday, I _____.

Now You Try!   CheckLink   DL 261 ~ 264   CD3-77 ~ CD3-80

質問とそれに対する 3 つの応答を聞いて、最も適切なものを選びましょう。

1. (A) (B) (C)   **2.** (A) (B) (C)   **3.** (A) (B) (C)   **4.** (A) (B) (C)

Part 3 Conversations 【会話問題】

Part 3 では 3 人の話し手による会話も出題されます（会話が流れる前に "Questions 1 through 3 refer to the following conversation **with three speakers**." とアナウンスされます）。質問では人物の名前が挙げられるかもしれないので、覚えておくようにしましょう。

Warming Up   CheckLink   DL 265 ~266   CD3-81 ~ CD3-82

音声を聞いて空所の語句を書き取り、質問に対する最も適切な答えを選びましょう。

M1: The ¹_____ for our project is July 31. That's this ²_____.
 W: That's right, Tom. We're behind schedule because we're still waiting for some ³_____ from the head office. Any ideas, Gary?
M2: Yes, I'll talk to the ⁴_____ and ask for a few more ⁵_____.

1. When is the deadline for the project?
   (A) Tuesday   (B) Wednesday   (C) Thursday   (D) Friday

2. Why is the project behind schedule?
   (A) The project leader is on a business trip.   (B) The weather was bad.
   (C) A machine stopped working.   (D) They do not have some information.

3. What will Gary do?

 (A) Make a new plan   (B) Ask the manager for more time

 (C) Hire more workers   (D) Take short lunch breaks

 **Now You Try!**    CheckLink   DL 267 ~ 270   CD3-83 ~ CD3-86

会話を聞いて、質問に対する最も適切な答えを選びましょう。

Conversation 1

1. What will people bring to the meeting?

 (A) Their designs

 (B) Their computers

 (C) Their ID cards

 (D) Their lunch

2. How long is the meeting?

 (A) One hour

 (B) Two hours

 (C) Three hours

 (D) Four hours

3. Who will the man meet in the afternoon?

 (A) A travel agent

 (B) A friend

 (C) A customer

 (D) A project team

Conversation 2

4. Who is the woman?

 (A) A company president

 (B) A systems engineer

 (C) A financial planner

 (D) A department manager

5. What are the speakers discussing?

 (A) Office hours

 (B) A project

 (C) A bonus system

 (D) Business trips

6. What does Henry think about the system?

 (A) It will save money.

 (B) It will save time.

 (C) It will help the president.

 (D) It will give more motivation.

Part 4 Talks   【説明文問題】

"May I have your attention, please?" のように、注意を引く発言に気をつけましょう。次の
発言に答えに関係する重要な情報が含まれているかもしれません。

 **Warming Up**   CheckLink   DL 271 ~ 272   CD3-87 ~ CD3-88

音声を聞いて空所の語句を書き取り、質問に対する最も適切な答えを選びましょう。

May I have everyone's ¹＿＿＿＿＿? Some members are on business ²＿＿＿＿＿,
and two members are on ³＿＿＿＿＿. So, I've decided to ⁴＿＿＿＿＿ today's
meeting. We'll have it on Thursday ⁵＿＿＿＿＿. I'll tell you the meeting time
tomorrow. Please check your ⁶＿＿＿＿＿.

1. Who most likely is the speaker?

(A) A customer

(B) An office manager

(C) A travel agent

(D) A bus driver

2. Why has the speaker canceled the meeting?

(A) Some members are not available.

(B) She will be on a business trip.

(C) Some equipment is not working.

(D) Some data is not ready.

3. What will the listeners do tomorrow?

(A) Check some data

(B) Write reports

(C) Read an e-mail

(D) Attend a meeting

Now You Try!

CheckLink  DL 273 ~ 276 CD3-89 ~ CD3-92

説明文を聞いて、質問に対する最も適切な答えを選びましょう。

Talk 1

1. What is the topic of the talk?

(A) A new office building

(B) Office cleaning

(C) Old equipment

(D) Worker safety

2. What will workers need to enter and leave the building?

(A) A key

(B) Their smartphones

(C) Their access cards

(D) An ID number

3. What will Ben Ramsey do?

(A) Take employees' pictures

(B) Collect old ID cards

(C) Explain the new system

(D) Give workers a new key

Talk 2

4. What is the speaker announcing?

(A) A company event

(B) New office rules

(C) A vacation policy

(D) The opening of a new branch

5. Where does the speaker work?

(A) In a bank

(B) In a school

(C) In a library

(D) In a fitness center

6. Why should employees see the speaker?

(A) To receive their bonuses

(B) To sign a contract

(C) To get information

(D) To discuss their schedules

Vocabulary Builder B

CheckLink DL 277 CD3-93

次の1～8の意味に合うものをa～hから選びましょう。その後で、音声を聞いて答えを確認しましょう。

1. proposal （　） 　　**2.** submit （　） 　　**3.** management （　） 　　**4.** on time （　）

5. away （　） 　　**6.** complete （　） 　　**7.** on business （　） 　　**8.** guard （　）

a. 時間通りに	**b.** 完成する、完全な 　　**c.** 提案 　　**d.** 提出する
e. 経営（陣）	**f.** 仕事で 　　**g.** 離れて 　　**h.** 守衛、警備員

Part 5　Sentence Completion 　　【短文穴埋め問題】

接続詞の種類と意味を覚えて、2つのものをつないだ場合に意味が通じるのはどれかを考えるようにしましょう。

等位接続詞　「語と語」「句と句」「節と節」をつなぐ場合に使います。

and「…と」	*sunny and hot*（晴れて暑い）
or「…または」	*in the morning or at night*（午前中か夜に）
but「…だけど」	*difficult but interesting*（難しいけれどおもしろい）
so「…なので」	*It's a nice day, so I'll go for a walk.*（天気がいいので散歩に行きます）

従属接続詞　「節と節」をつなぐ場合に使います。

before「…する前に」 after「…する後に」	*Call me before you leave.*（出発する前に電話してください） *Let's have tea after we study.*（勉強してからお茶にしましょう）
because「…なので」 although「…だけれど」	*I'm happy because I passed the test.* （試験に合格したのでうれしいです） *Although it was hot, we enjoyed the picnic.* （暑かったけれども、私たちはピクニックを楽しみました）
when「…するとき」 while「…している間に」	*Babies cry when they're hungry.* （赤ちゃんは空腹のときに泣きます） *He called me while I was sleeping.* （私が寝ている間に彼は私に電話をかけてきました）
if「もし…なら」 unless「もし…でないなら」	*Put on a sweater if you're cold.*（寒いならセーターを着なさい） *I'll walk home unless it rains.*（雨が降らなければ歩いて帰ります）

Warming Up

CheckLink

正しい選択肢を選び、文を完成させましょう。

1. I put cream (**a.** and　**b.** but) sugar in my tea.
2. He has a car, (**a.** but　**b.** so) he doesn't drive.
3. Lock the door (**a.** if　**b.** although) you go out.
4. I'm tired (**a.** because　**b.** ,so) I'll go to bed.

Now You Try!

CheckLink

4つの選択肢から最も適切なものを選び、文を完成させましょう。

1. ------- the new office opens, we will have a party.
   (A) After　　(B) Although　　(C) So　　(D) But

2. Ms. Williams will help us ------- Mr. Stewart is away on business.
   (A) and　　(B) after　　(C) so　　(D) while

3. No one can enter the office ------- they show their ID card.
   (A) because　　(B) if　　(C) so　　(D) unless

4. John canceled the presentation ------- some equipment was not working.
   (A) although　　(B) so　　(C) because　　(D) but

5. There is good communication between management ------- staff.
   (A) and　　(B) or　　(C) but　　(D) so

6. The manager will explain the schedule ------- Mr. Conners arrives at the office.
   (A) although　　(B) because　　(C) when　　(D) while

7. Several new offices will open next year, ------- the River Street office will close.
   (A) because　　(B) but　　(C) before　　(D) or

8. Kay Wells will be the new office manager, -------- Bob Kane will be her assistant.
   (A) before　　(B) and　　(C) or　　(D) because

Part 6 Text Completion 【長文穴埋め問題】

選択肢の複数の接続詞が空所に当てはまりそうな場合は、前後の文を読んで意味を理解しましょう。

Warming Up

ⓒ CheckLink

正しい選択肢を選び、文を完成させましょう。

1. Please show me the proposal (**a.** before **b.** after) you send it. I want to check it first.

2. Employees must show their ID cards (**a.** before **b.** after) they enter the building. A guard in the lobby will check them.

3. We will have a meeting with Bill (**a.** when **b.** unless) he finishes his report. He will finish it around 4:00.

4. Carol is in the office today. Let's talk to her about the project (**a.** if **b.** while) she's here.

Now You Try!

ⓒ CheckLink

4 つの選択肢から最も適切なものを選び、文を完成させましょう。

Questions 1–4 refer to the following memo.

> I need to do two things ------- I submit my sales report. First, I need to double-check
> **1.**
>
> the data. I am also waiting for some sales information from our stores. -------. Can
> **2.**
>
> you change the ------- to August 20? I'm sorry for the -------.
> **3.** **4.**

1. (A) while   (B) after   (C) because   (D) before

2. (A) There is a long line.   (B) I expect to receive it tomorrow.
   (C) Their store hours are different.   (D) It was very surprising news.

3. (A) deadline   (B) law   (C) subject   (D) calendar

4. (A) accident   (B) delay   (C) mistake   (D) service

Part 7 Reading Comprehension 【読解問題】

よく使われるビジネスフレーズが文書にも選択肢にも登場するので、そのような表現をできるだけたくさん覚えましょう。

Warming Up

CheckLink

次の 1~6 の意味を a~f から選びましょう。

1. work overtime (　　)　　**2.** meet the deadline (　　)　　**3.** hand in (　　)

4. cut costs (　　)　　**5.** save time (　　)　　**6.** free of charge (　　)

a. 無料で	**b.** 残業する	**c.** 費用を削減する
d. 時間を節約する	**e.** 提出する	**f.** 期限に間に合う

Now You Try!

CheckLink

文書を読んで、設問に対する最も適切な答えを選びましょう。

Questions 1–3 refer to the following memo.

MEMO

To: All employees
From: Greg Wu, General Manager

On January 10, we will switch to a new paperless reporting system. Please install the new software between January 5 and 9. With the software, you can see your work schedule and request holidays. This new system will save time and cut costs. Please e-mail me if you have any questions.

---

1. What is the purpose of the memo?

(A) To explain a report

(B) To tell workers about new office hours

(C) To report a problem

(D) To announce a new system

2. What should employees do before January 10?

(A) Stop using paper   (B) Install software   (C) Read a report   (D) E-mail Mr. Wu

3. What is NOT stated about the new system?

(A) It will reduce costs.

(B) It does not require paper.

(C) It is safe.

(D) It will save time.

Questions 4–6 refer to the following e-mail.

To:	Project members
From:	Jake Daniels
Date:	March 17
Subject:	Project is done

Many thanks to all of you for your hard work on the project. It was a very busy two months, and everyone worked overtime every day. But because of your great effort, we could meet the deadline. I gave the report to our company president this morning.

Thanks again. I look forward to our next project together.

Jake

4. What is the purpose of the e-mail?

(A) To schedule a meeting

(B) To request ideas

(C) To discuss a deadline

(D) To thank co-workers

5. What did the project members do?

(A) They cut costs.

(B) They saved time.

(C) They met the deadline.

(D) They worked free of change.

6. What did Mr. Daniels do this morning?

(A) He wrote a report.

(B) He handed in a document.

(C) He called a customer.

(D) He gave a present to everyone.

Computers & Technology

トピック　コンピューター&テクノロジー　文法　能動態・受動態

Vocabulary Builder

CheckLink　DL 278　CD4-02

次の 1 ～ 8 の意味に合うものを a ～ h から選びましょう。その後で、音声を聞いて答えを確認しましょう。

1. factory （　） 　　**2.** allow （　） 　　**3.** update （　） 　　**4.** protect （　）

5. develop （　） 　　**6.** monitor （　） 　　**7.** automatic （　） 　　**8.** virtual （　）

a. 保護する	**b.** 発展させる	**c.** 工場	**d.** モニター、監視する
e. 仮想の、事実上の	**f.** 更新（する）	**g.** 自動の	**h.** 許す

Part 1 Photographs 【写真描写問題】

写真に写っている物が聞こえたからといって単純にその文を選ばずに、動詞や前置詞が写真の物と合っているか確認するようにしましょう。

Warming Up

CheckLink　DL 279　CD4-03

音声を聞いて空所の語句を書き取り、写真を最も適切に描写しているものを選びましょう。

(A) She's ＿＿＿＿＿ a ＿＿＿＿＿.

(B) She's ＿＿＿＿＿ on the ＿＿＿＿＿.

(C) She's ＿＿＿＿＿ a ＿＿＿＿＿.

(D) She's ＿＿＿＿＿ a ＿＿＿＿＿.

Now You Try!

CheckLink　DL 280 ～ 281　CD4-04 ～ CD4-05

写真を描写する 4 つの音声を聞いて、最も適切なものを選びましょう。

❶

Ⓐ Ⓑ Ⓒ Ⓓ

❷

Ⓐ Ⓑ Ⓒ Ⓓ

Part 2 Question-Response 【応答問題】

Part 2 では質問だけでなく、"Can I …?" や "May I …?" などを使って「…してもいいですか」と許可を求めたり、"Can you …?" や "Would you …?" などを使って「…してもらえますか」と依頼をしたりすることもあります。

Warming Up   CheckLink   DL 282 ~ 283   CD4-06 ~ CD4-07

音声を聞いて空所の語句を書き取り、質問に対する最も適切な応答を選びましょう。

1. May I see inside your factory?
   - (A) Yes, I ＿＿＿＿＿＿ it.
   - (B) Copy ＿＿＿＿＿＿.
   - (C) Yes, please ＿＿＿＿＿＿ me.

2. Can you take a look at my computer?
   - (A) No, I ＿＿＿＿＿＿ one.
   - (B) ＿＿＿＿＿＿ the problem?
   - (C) A ＿＿＿＿＿＿.

Now You Try!   CheckLink   DL 284 ~ 287   CD4-08 ~ CD4-11

質問とそれに対する 3 つの応答を聞いて、最も適切なものを選びましょう。

1. (A) (B) (C)   2. (A) (B) (C)   3. (A) (B) (C)   4. (A) (B) (C)

Part 3 Conversations 【会話問題】

"Do you need help?" や "Can you explain the problem?" のように、申し出や依頼が会話に登場する場合もあります。こうした文が聞こえたら、相手がどのように返事をするか注意して聞きましょう。

Warming Up   CheckLink   DL 288 ~ 289   CD4-12 ~ CD4-13

音声を聞いて空所の語句を書き取り、質問に対する最も適切な答えを選びましょう。

> M: Here's a ^{1} ＿＿＿＿＿＿ of equipment in Room A. Do you need anything else for your ^{2} ＿＿＿＿＿＿ tomorrow?
>
> W: Well, since there will be ^{3} ＿＿＿＿＿＿ people, it would be ^{4} ＿＿＿＿＿＿ to have a ^{5} ＿＿＿＿＿＿.

1. What does the man show the woman?
   - (A) A list
   - (B) An outline
   - (C) A box
   - (D) A catalog

2. What will the woman do tomorrow?
   - (A) Go to a factory
   - (B) Attend a meeting
   - (C) Have a party
   - (D) Make a presentation

3. What will the man get for the woman?

    (A) A whiteboard   (B) A projector   (C) A microphone   (D) A pointer

🔲 Now You Try!   ↻CheckLink   🎧 DL 290 ~ 293   ◉CD4-14 ~ ◉CD4-17

会話を聞いて、質問に対する最も適切な答えを選びましょう。

Conversation 1

1. Why does the woman call the man?
    (A) To make an appointment
    (B) To report a computer problem
    (C) To check on an order
    (D) To request a catalog

2. What information does the man want?
    (A) A telephone number
    (B) An address
    (C) A password
    (D) An ID number

3. What will the man do?
    (A) Visit the woman's office
    (B) Send an e-mail
    (C) Make a telephone call
    (D) Contact a support worker

Conversation 2

4. Where do the speakers most likely work?
    (A) At a cosmetics company
    (B) At a library
    (C) At a station
    (D) At a hotel

5. What are the speakers discussing?
    (A) A machine
    (B) A new advertisement
    (C) A new product
    (D) A mirror

6. What do customers receive?
    (A) Free downloads
    (B) Automatic updates
    (C) Special discounts
    (D) Virtual experiences

Part 4 Talks   【説明文問題】

会社名は TipTop Clothing Company のように「会社名＋業種を表す語句」で登場することがよくあります。後半が聞き取れれば何の会社かわかるので、内容についていきやすくなります。

🔲 Warming Up   ↻CheckLink   🎧 DL 294 ~ 295   ◉CD4-18 ~ ◉CD4-19

音声を聞いて空所の語句を書き取り、質問に対する最も適切な答えを選びましょう。

Hello, I'm Ron Woods from Filmore Computers. Today, I'm going to talk about technology in the [1]_____. Technology is a powerful [2]_____. It can change the way we work and [3]_____. It allows us to [4]_____ better technologies. After my [5]_____, I'll be happy to answer your [6]_____.

1. What is the topic of the talk?

   (A) Technology in business   (B) Technology in schools

   (C) Dangerous technologies   (D) Future Technologies

2. What does the speaker say about technology?

   (A) It is convenient.   (B) It is difficult.

   (C) It is a powerful tool.   (D) It controls our lives.

3. What will there be after the talk?

   (A) A presentation   (B) A panel discussion

   (C) Q&A   (D) A lunch

Now You Try!

 CheckLink   DL 296 ~ 299   CD4-20 ~ CD4-23

説明文を聞いて、質問に対する最も適切な答えを選びましょう。

Talk 1

1. What is Fix Technologies?

   (A) A computer company

   (B) A delivery company

   (C) An IT support company

   (D) A home safety company

2. Who will be the company's customers?

   (A) College students

   (B) Small business owners

   (C) Large companies

   (D) Tourists

3. What will listeners see on the company's Web site?

   (A) A list of prices

   (B) The company profile

   (C) Customer comments

   (D) A list of services

Talk 2

4. What will the company do during the weekend?

   (A) Check for problems

   (B) Install a new software program

   (C) Delete old files

   (D) Update its Web site

5. What is the purpose of the company's action?

   (A) To save money

   (B) To protect online data

   (C) To make better products

   (D) To help customers

6. What will happen on Monday morning?

   (A) A training session

   (B) An office meeting

   (C) A presentation

   (D) A security check

Vocabulary Builder B

 CheckLink　DL 300　CD4-24

次の1〜8の意味に合うものをa〜hから選びましょう。その後で、音声を聞いて答えを確認しましょう。

1. engineer（　）　**2.** app（　）　**3.** operate（　）　**4.** production（　）

5. mobile（　）　**6.** collaboration（　）　**7.** strength（　）　**8.** turn off（　）

a.（電気などを）消す	**b.** 操作する、作動する	**c.** 技術者	**d.** アプリケーション
e. 生産	**f.** 携帯電話の、モバイルの	**g.** 協力、共同作業	**h.** 強み

Part 5　Sentence Completion　【短文穴埋め問題】

主語が動作を行っているのか、それとも動作を受けているのかを考えて、能動態と受動態を見分けましょう。

能動態

● 「AがBをする」というように、主語が動作を行います。英語の一般的な文はこの形をしています。

受動態

● 「AがBをされる」というように、主語が動作を受けます。動作を強調したり、動作を行う人が不明か重要でなかったりする場合に使います。
● 受動態は〈be動詞＋過去分詞〉という形をしています。
● 動作を行う人を表す場合はbyを使います。

	能動態	受動態
現在時制	*Bees **make** honey.* （ミツバチはハチミツを作ります） *Meg **teaches** the children.* （メグは子どもたちに教えます）	*Honey **is made** by bees.* （ハチミツはミツバチによって作られます） *The children **are taught** by Meg.* （子どもたちはメグによって教えられます）
過去時制	*Tom **drew** this picture.* （トムがこの絵を描きました） *Sue **washed** the dishes.* （スーがお皿を洗いました）	*This picture **was drawn** by Tom.* （この絵はトムによって描かれました） *The dishes **were washed** by Sue.* （お皿はスーによって洗われました）

Warming Up

次の文を1と2は能動態に、3と4は受動態に変えて書いてみましょう。

1. Furniture is made by the company. _____

2. These letters were written by Sally. _____

3. Many people watch this TV program. _____

4. The children ate all the cookies. _____

Now You Try!

↻ CheckLink

4つの選択肢から最も適切なものを選び、文を完成させましょう。

1. Gold Air ------- the best safety equipment.
   (A) are used   (B) uses   (C) is used   (D) using

2. These mobile phones ------- by a team of engineers.
   (A) makes   (B) make   (C) were made   (D) were making

3. Day & Night Fashion ------- its Web site every week.
   (A) updating   (B) updates   (C) is updated   (D) was updated

4. TrueFit Company software ------- for small businesses.
   (A) designs   (B) designing   (C) is designed   (D) is designing

5. Robot waiters ------- the customers in this restaurant.
   (A) are served   (B) serving   (C) is served   (D) serve

6. The company recently ------- new software on all its computers.
   (A) installed   (B) installing   (C) is installed   (D) was installed

7. Vana Computers -------- by Marlene Technologies Company.
   (A) was bought   (B) bought   (C) buying   (D) buy

8. Delray mobile phones ------- in more than 50 countries around the world.
   (A) sells   (B) is sold   (C) selling   (D) are sold

Part **6** Text Completion 【長文穴埋め問題】

文は前の文との関係を示す語句で始まることがあります。以下のような表現を覚えましょう。

as a result（結果として）	for example（例えば）	however（けれども）
in addition（加えて）	in fact（実際に）	instead（代わりに）
finally（ついに）	therefore（したがって）	otherwise（さもなければ）

Warming Up   CheckLink

正しい選択肢を選び、文を完成させましょう。

1. Computers don't always work perfectly. ¹(**a.** For example   **b.** Instead), sometimes the screen freezes. ²(**a.** Otherwise   **b.** As a result), you sometimes lose information.

2. Smartphones are very common in the United States. ¹(**a.** In fact   **b.** Finally), about 96% of Americans between 18 and 49 have a smartphone. ²(**a.** Otherwise **b.** However), only about 60% of Americans over 65 own one.

Now You Try! CheckLink

4 つの選択肢から最も適切なものを選び、文を完成させましょう。

Questions 1–4 refer to the following article.

> DENVER (July 3)—Walco's Shoes plans to build a ------- factory in Denver,
> 1.
> Colorado. -------. According to the maker, the robots can operate twenty-four
> 2.
> hours a day. -------, they can easily make shoes in different sizes. The factory will
> 3.
> begin ------- in June next year.
> 4.

NOTE according to … …によると

1. (A) clever   (B) labor   (C) modern   (D) wise

2. (A) The factory opened yesterday.   (B) The company makes sports shoes.
   (C) The shoes will be 100% handmade. (D) The shoes will be made by robots.

3. (A) Otherwise   (B) However   (C) In addition   (D) Instead

4. (A) produce   (B) production   (C) productivity   (D) productively

Part 7 Reading Comprehension 【読解問題】

文が難しくてわからないときは、わかる単語や前後の文の流れから意味を推測してみましょう。また、多くの場合、選択肢ではやさしく言い換えられていることも覚えておきましょう。

Warming Up ⟳CheckLink

次の 1~4 の文を言い換えたものを a~d から選びましょう。

1. I booked it on the Internet. ( )
2. I shut down my laptop. ( )
3. The printer won't print the document. ( )
4. This place has a wireless hotspot. ( )

> **a.** The machine is not working. **b.** I reserved it online.
>
> **c.** Wi-Fi is available here. **d.** I turned off my computer.

Now You Try! ⟳CheckLink

文書を読んで、設問に対する最も適切な答えを選びましょう。

Questions 1–3 refer to the following advertisement.

Better Truck Routes, Better Business

Helix GPS Systems is helping truck drivers around the world. With our system, you can:

- ✓ Hear voice directions and change the navigation voice.
- ✓ Preview the map. You will find convenience stores, restaurants, gas stations, etc.
- ✓ Receive updates on roads.
- ✓ Download maps.

> **For more information and prices, visit helixgpssystems.com**

---

1. What is the advertisement for?
   (A) A security system (B) A camera
   (C) A computer game (D) A navigation system

2. What is on the preview map?
   (A) Street names (B) Gas stations
   (C) 3-D images (D) Road signs

3. What does the system give users?

(A) Opening times of gas stations

(B) News from around the world

(C) Information about streets

(D) A choice of languages for voice directions

Questions 4–6 refer to the following article.

SILICON VALLEY, California — June 5 —

A-Plus Computers and Staple Technologies have announced a tie-up. The new Mobile Office System app will use the strengths of both companies. A-Plus makes high-performance computers. Staple has had great success with its mobile apps. Together, the companies will create apps for businesses. The apps will be available in early September.

4. What is the article about?

(A) A collaboration between two companies

(B) A new mobile phone

(C) A marketing idea

(D) The sale of a technology company

5. What is A-Plus Computers' strength?

(A) Its low cost

(B) Its large selection of models

(C) Its customer service

(D) Its excellent computers

6. What will the two companies create together?

(A) Mobile devices

(B) A new company

(C) Apps

(D) Tablet computers

Unit 14 Events

トピック イベント 文法 比較級・最上級

Vocabulary Builder (A)

CheckLink DL 301 CD4-25

次の 1 ～ 8 の意味に合うものを a ～ h から選びましょう。その後で、音声を聞いて答えを確認しましょう。

1. reception ( )　　**2.** conference ( )　　**3.** workshop ( )　　**4.** take place ( )
5. charity ( )　　**6.** guest ( )　　　**7.** invitation ( )　　**8.** register for ( )

a. 歓迎会、受付	b. 招待（状）	c. 慈善	d. 登録する
e. （大きな）会議	f. 行われる	g. 研修会	h. ゲスト、招待客

Part 1 Photographs 【写真描写問題】

写真の中で焦点が当てられていると思われる人物を正しく表す文を聞き取りましょう。聞く前に、キーワードとなりそうなものを予測してみましょう。

Warming Up

CheckLink DL 302 CD4-26

音声を聞いて空所の語句を書き取り、写真を最も適切に描写しているものを選びましょう。

(A) They're _____ _____ _____.

(B) One of the men is _____ _____
_____.

(C) One of the women is _____ _____.

(D) One of the men is _____ _____
_____.

Now You Try!

CheckLink DL 303 ~ 304 CD4-27 ~ CD4-28

写真を描写する 4 つの音声を聞いて、最も適切なものを選びましょう。

❶

Ⓐ Ⓑ Ⓒ Ⓓ

❷

Ⓐ Ⓑ Ⓒ Ⓓ

Part 2   Question-Response 【応答問題】

Part 2 では "Let's …" や "How about …?" "Why don't you …?" などを使って「…しましょう」「…しませんか」と提案をしたり、"Do you want to …?" や "Would you like to …?" を使って「…したいですか」と勧誘をしたりすることもあります。

Warming Up   CheckLink   DL 305 ~ 306   CD4-29 ~ CD4-30

音声を聞いて空所の語句を書き取り、質問に対する最も適切な応答を選びましょう。

1. Do you want to have lunch after the talk?
   (A) Yes, it's Italian _____ .
   (B) Not very _____ .
   (C) Sorry, I have other _____ .

2. Let's register for the conference.
   (A) OK, we can do it _____ .
   (B) It's a _____ conference.
   (C) For three _____ .

Now You Try!   CheckLink   DL 307 ~ 310   CD4-31 ~ CD4-34

質問とそれに対する 3 つの応答を聞いて、最も適切なものを選びましょう。

1. Ⓐ Ⓑ Ⓒ   2. Ⓐ Ⓑ Ⓒ   3. Ⓐ Ⓑ Ⓒ   4. Ⓐ Ⓑ Ⓒ

Part 3   Conversations 【会話問題】

"Of course." や "My pleasure." (喜んで)、"I'm afraid not." (残念ながら) といった短い応答を聞き取ると、相手の言ったことに対してどのように応じたかがわかり、会話の流れについていきやすくなります。

Warming Up   CheckLink   DL 311 ~312   CD4-35 ~ CD4-36

音声を聞いて空所の語句を書き取り、質問に対する最も適切な答えを選びましょう。

> W: Tim, are your wife and children coming to the company ¹_____?
> M: I'm afraid not. My wife ²_____ on Saturdays, and my kids have soccer ³_____ .
> M: Didn't you hear? It's on ⁴_____ ⁵_____ this year.

1. What are the speakers discussing?
   (A) A concert   (B) A game   (C) A party   (D) A picnic

2. What does the man's wife do on Saturdays?
   (A) Work   (B) Play a sport   (C) Take a class   (D) Babysit

3. When is the event this year?
   (A) Saturday afternoon   (B) Saturday night   (C) Sunday afternoon   (D) Sunday night

Now You Try!

CheckLink DL 313 ~ 316 CD4-37 ~ CD4-40

会話を聞いて、質問に対する最も適切な答えを選びましょう。

Conversation 1

1. Who most likely are the speakers?
(A) Dentists
(B) Chefs
(C) Teachers
(D) Web designers

2. What did the woman do?
(A) She registered for an event.
(B) She made a hotel reservation.
(C) She canceled an appointment.
(D) She prepared for a presentation.

3. What does the man want to see?
(A) Books
(B) Designs
(C) Furniture
(D) Equipment

Conversation 2

4. What kind of company does the man work for?
(A) A wedding company
(B) A food service company
(C) A cleaning company
(D) An entertainment company

5. Where will the event take place?
(A) At a restaurant
(B) At a museum
(C) At a company
(D) At a concert hall

6. What will the man send the woman?
(A) A price list
(B) A map
(C) A menu
(D) An invitation

Part 4 Talks 【説明文問題】

トークの中には話し手が行った行動の順番を説明するものもあります。それぞれの順番をイメージしながらトークについていきましょう。

Warming Up

CheckLink DL 317 ~ 318 CD4-41 ~ CD4-42

音声を聞いて空所の語句を書き取り、質問に対する最も適切な答えを選びましょう。

Hello, Dr. Hawkins. This is Lynn Evans from Pines *1*_____ Center. I've just *2*_____ you an *3*_____ with the plan for your *4*_____. Could you please *5*_____ the plan? After that, I'll *6*_____ the room for you. Thank you.

1. Where does the speaker work?
   (A) At a shopping center
   (B) At a conference center
   (C) At a sports center
   (D) At an arts center

2. What has the speaker sent to Dr. Hawkins?
   (A) A card
   (B) A picture
   (C) A link to a Web page
   (D) An e-mail

3. What will Dr. Hawkins probably do?
   (A) Check a plan
   (B) Send a guest list
   (C) Make a payment
   (D) Change the schedule

Now You Try!

 CheckLink DL 319 ~ 322 CD4-43 ~ CD4-46

説明文を聞いて、質問に対する最も適切な答えを選びましょう。

Talk 1

1. Where is the speaker?
   (A) At a concert hall
   (B) At an art gallery
   (C) At a newspaper company
   (D) At a university

2. What was Mr. Tomlinson's job?
   (A) Artist
   (B) Photographer
   (C) Pilot
   (D) Professor

3. What are Mr. Tomlinson's books about?
   (A) People
   (B) Historical events
   (C) Places
   (D) Fashion trends

Talk 2

4. Where is the speaker?
   (A) At a speech contest
   (B) At a birthday party
   (C) At a school
   (D) At a dinner event

5. What will the money from the event help?
   (A) A library
   (B) A city zoo
   (C) A hospital
   (D) A museum

6. What is the entertainment?
   (A) A dance performance
   (B) A concert
   (C) A magic show
   (D) A bingo game

Vocabulary Builder (B)

CheckLink   DL 323   CD4-47

次の 1 ～ 8 の意味に合うものを a ～ h から選びましょう。その後で、音声を聞いて答えを確認しましょう。

1. festival (　　)　　　**2.** annual (　　)　　　**3.** seminar (　　)　　　**4.** hold (　　)

5. useful (　　)　　**6.** opening ceremony (　　)　　**7.** city hall (　　)　　**8.** celebration (　　)

a. 開会式、開幕式	**b.** お祝い、祝賀会	**c.** 開催する	**d.** セミナー
e. 毎年恒例の	**f.** 祭	**g.** 市役所	**h.** 役に立つ

Part 5 Sentence Completion 【短文穴埋め問題】

比較級や最上級が選択肢にあるのを見たら、比較されているものの数を考えて比較級と最上級のルールを当てはめましょう。

比較級

● 2 つのものを比べる場合に使います。
● 短い形容詞・副詞の場合は語尾に er をつけます（不規則なものもあります）。
● 比較級の後ろに than をつけて比較の対象を表すこともよくあります。

*Mike is **older** than Ken. / Yesterday was hot, but today is **hotter**.*

最上級

● 3 つ以上のものを比べる場合に使います。
● 短い形容詞・副詞の場合は語尾に est をつけます（不規則なものもあります）。
● 一般的に最上級の前には the をつけます。

*He runs the **fastest** in his class. / The elephant is the **largest** land animal on earth.*

原級	比較級	最上級
fast	fast**er**	(the) fast**est**
large	larg**er**	(the) larg**est**
hot	hot**ter**	(the) hot**test**
healthy	health**ier**	(the) health**iest**
good/well	**better**	(the) **best**
bad	**worse**	(the) **worst**
far	**farther/further**	(the) **farthest/furthest**

● 長い形容詞や副詞の場合、比較級には more、最上級には most を前につけます。

*Peaches are **more expensive** than bananas. / She drives the **most carefully**.*

原級	比較級	最上級
expensive	**more** expensive	**most** expensive
carefully	**more** carefully	**most** carefully

Warming Up

CheckLink

正しい選択肢を選び、文を完成させましょう。

1. Ben is (**a.** taller   **b.** the tallest) than Tom.
2. New York is big, but Tokyo is (**a.** bigger   **b.** bigger than).
3. The Giants are the (**a.** worse   **b.** worst) team of all this year.
4. This is (**a.** more beautiful than   **b.** the most beautiful) park in the city.

Now You Try!

CheckLink

4 つの選択肢から最も適切なものを選び、文を完成させましょう。

1. The summer festival is ------- than the winter festival.
   (A) popular   (B) popularly   (C) more popular   (D) most popular

2. The Rocky City marathon race is the ------- event of the year.
   (A) largest   (B) largely   (C) most largely   (D) larger

3. Don Lang is always the ------- speaker at the company's parties.
   (A) funny   (B) funnier   (C) fun   (D) funniest

4. Tomorrow will be ------- than today, so it will be perfect for the company hike.
   (A) warmer   (B) warm   (C) warmest   (D) warmly

5. The company will hold its conference in the ------- hall in the city.
   (A) newest   (B) newer   (C) more newly   (D) most newly

6. The Valley Park Charity Concert gets bigger and ------- every year.
   (A) good   (B) well   (C) better   (D) best

7. Max Foods will hold its food festival two weeks ------- than last year.
   (A) late   (B) latest   (C) lately   (D) later

8. The ---------- French designer showed his collection at the fashion show.
   (A) greatly   (B) greater   (C) greatest   (D) greatness

Part 6 | Text Completion 【長文穴埋め問題】

選択肢の文が前の文との関係を示す語句（p.126）で始まっている場合、前の文を読んで2つの文の意味がつながるかを考えましょう。

 Warming Up ↻ CheckLink

正しい選択肢を選び、文を完成させましょう。

1. The company's summer picnic has been canceled. (**a.** As a result, only a few people attended. **b.** Instead, an autumn barbecue will be held.)

2. The workshop is free. (**a.** In fact, it is an annual event. **b.** However, there are seats for only 25 people.)

3. Each presenter spoke for 15 minutes. (**a.** Finally, the main speaker gave her speech. **b.** For example, some people did not have tickets.)

Now You Try! ↻ CheckLink

4つの選択肢から最も適切なものを選び、文を完成させましょう。

Questions 1–4 refer to the following letter.

Dear Ms. Langston,

Thank you for your speech at our seminar yesterday. You gave a very interesting
and ------- talk. -------. And thank you for talking with some of the workers after the
    1.   **2.**
seminar. I think they will work ------- now. Good luck with your ------- at the
            3.   **4.**
conference in San Diego next week.

Kindest regards,

Stan Franklin

---

1. (A) use   (B) usefulness   (C) useful   (D) usefully

2. (A) However, I was unable to attend the seminar.
   (B) In fact, I learned many things from you.
   (C) Otherwise, it was excellent.
   (D) In addition, a small party was held.

3. (A) harder   (B) hardly   (C) hardness   (D) hardest

4. (A) present   (B) presents   (C) presenter   (D) presentation

Part **7** | Reading Comprehension 【読解問題】

複数の文書に関する質問の中には、"In the e-mail"（Eメールで）や "According to the notice"（お知らせによると）のように、どの文書を読めば答えが見つかるかを教えてくれるものもあります。時間の節約になるので見逃さないようにしましょう。

Warming Up

CheckLink

次の２つの文書を読んで質問に答えましょう。

Notice: Beach Cleanup

Our volunteer cleanup at Bandy Beach will be on Saturday, August 31. We'll start at 10:30 A.M. and finish around noon. Everyone is welcome. For more information, please contact Carol at cbixby@webuild.com

---

Dear Carol,

My name is Jerry Reed. I'm interested in volunteering for the beach cleanup, but I don't have a car. Will there be a bus service to the beach?

Sincerely yours,
Jerry Reed

---

1. According to the notice, what will volunteers do on August 31?

(A) Play with children

(B) Teach children

(C) Cook food

(D) Pick up trash

2. In the e-mail, what is Mr. Reed asking about?

(A) The size of a beach

(B) The number of volunteers

(C) A bus service

(D) Food

Now You Try!

C CheckLink

文書を読んで、設問に対する最も適切な答えを選びましょう。

Questions 1-5 refer to the following article and e-mail.

New City Hall Grand Opening

Crestland City will hold the grand opening of its new city hall on Fillmore Street. The city spent $200 million for it. The new city hall will give better service to the people of the city. The celebration will take place on Saturday, May 1 from 10 A.M. to 3 P.M. The opening ceremony will begin at noon.

From:	Virginia Morris
To:	Henry Baker
Date:	March 9
Subject:	Special invitation

Dear Mr. Baker:

Thank you for your 50 years of volunteer service in our city. We would like to invite you to the grand opening of the new city hall. After the ceremony, there will be a party for guests in the city hall garden. We hope that you will be able to attend both events.

Best wishes,

Virginia Morris
Crestland City Hall

---

1. According to the article, what can Crestland City people expect from the new city hall?

(A) More parking spaces

(B) Better service

(C) Great views

(D) Better security

2. Who is Henry Baker?

(A) A business owner　(B) A musician　(C) A volunteer worker　(D) A tour guide

3. What is planned for guests?

(A) A private concert　　　　　　(B) A special tour

(C) Lunch with Virginia Morris　　(D) A garden party

4. What is NOT mentioned about the new building?

(A) The cost　　(B) The location　　(C) The garden　　(D) The size

5. What will Mr. Baker probably do on May 1?

(A) Attend a ceremony　　　　　(B) Give a speech

(C) Give a tour of the city hall　　(D) Cut a cake

Sales & Marketing

トピック｜セールス＆マーケティング 　文法｜関係詞

Vocabulary Builder A

CheckLink 　DL 324 　CD4-48

次の１～８の意味に合うものをa～hから選びましょう。その後で、音声を聞いて答えを確認しましょう。

1. sales report（　　） 　**2.** advertising（　　） 　**3.** award（　　） 　**4.** budget（　　）

5. survey（　　） 　**6.** strategy（　　） 　**7.** region（　　） 　**8.** best-selling（　　）

a. 最も売れている	**b.** 予算	**c.** 調査（する）	**d.** 地域
e. 営業報告書	**f.** 戦略	**g.** 賞（を与える）	**h.** 宣伝（活動）

Part 1 Photographs 【写真描写問題】

これまで学んだすべてのタイプの問題を思い出してみましょう。それぞれの文を聞きながら頭の中でイメージして、写真に合うものを選びましょう。

Warming Up

CheckLink 　DL 325 　CD4-49

音声を聞いて空所の語句を書き取り、写真を最も適切に描写しているものを選びましょう。

(A) One of the men is _____ _____
_____.

(B) The woman is _____ _____ her
_____.

(C) One of the men is _____ _____
_____.

(D) The woman is _____ the driver's _____.

Now You Try!

CheckLink 　DL 326 ~ 327 　CD4-50 ~ 　CD4-51

写真を描写する４つの音声を聞いて、最も適切なものを選びましょう。

❶

Ⓐ Ⓑ Ⓒ Ⓓ

❷

Ⓐ Ⓑ Ⓒ Ⓓ

Part 2　Question-Response　　　【応答問題】

Part 2 では "This room is very hot." のように普通の文が出題されることもあります。状況を想像して、"The air conditioner isn't working." のように自分だったらどのような応答をするかを考えてみましょう。

▣ Warming Up　　CheckLink　DL 328 ~ 329　CD4-52 ~ CD4-53

音声を聞いて空所の語句を書き取り、質問に対する最も適切な応答を選びましょう。

1. Sales are up this month.
   (A) A great _____.
   (B) They're 30% _____.
   (C) May I see the sales _____?

2. Our new TV advertisement is a big hit.
   (A) It's very _____.
   (B) Especially among young _____.
   (C) OK, I'll call the _____.

▣ Now You Try!　　CheckLink　DL 330 ~ 333　CD4-54 ~ CD4-57

質問とそれに対する 3 つの応答を聞いて、最も適切なものを選びましょう。

1. Ⓐ Ⓑ Ⓒ　　2. Ⓐ Ⓑ Ⓒ　　3. Ⓐ Ⓑ Ⓒ　　4. Ⓐ Ⓑ Ⓒ

Part 3　Conversations　　　【会話問題】

売上や販売促進などに関する会話では、sales report、budget、cost、spend、best-sellingなどのキーワードに注意して、会社の商品や営業戦略とどのように関係しているか聞き取りましょう。

▣ Warming Up　　CheckLink　DL 334 ~335　CD4-58 ~ CD4-59

音声を聞いて空所の語句を書き取り、質問に対する最も適切な答えを選びましょう。

W: How much will 50 ^{1} _____ cost?
M: For 50, the ^{2} _____ will be $1,000.
W: Can you ^{3} _____ me a discount? I'll pay in ^{4} _____.
M: All right. You can have them for ^{5} _____.

1. What does the woman want to buy?
   (A) Sheets　　(B) Ties　　(C) T-shirts　　(D) Sweaters

2. What does the woman want to do?
   (A) Change an order　　　　　(B) Receive a discount
   (C) Increase her budget　　　(D) Buy the best-selling item

3. What will the woman do next?
   (A) Check the item　　(B) Pay the man　　(C) Call her boss　　(D) Send an e-mail

Now You Try!

CheckLink   DL 336 ~ 339   CD4-60 ~ CD4-63

会話を聞いて、質問に対する最も適切な答えを選びましょう。

Conversation 1

1. What are the best-selling items?
(A) Travel bags
(B) Shoulder bags
(C) Handbags
(D) Business bags

2. What is the most popular color?
(A) Black
(B) Navy
(C) Red
(D) Orange

3. Why is the woman surprised?
(A) Many customers are men.
(B) Some items are sold out.
(C) Orange is not a popular color.
(D) There are few young customers.

Conversation 2

4. What are the speakers discussing?
(A) A product
(B) A sales report
(C) A budget
(D) An event

5. What will be the company focus?
(A) Social media
(B) Television advertising
(C) Brand collaborations
(D) Radio advertising

6. What does the woman think about the plan?
(A) It will cost too much.
(B) It is unique.
(C) It is a bad strategy.
(D) It is very good.

Part 4 Talks 【説明文問題】

Part 4 でも図表問題は出題されます。Look at the graphic. で始まる質問がどのような情報を尋ねているかを頭に入れてから音声を聞いて、図表の情報と結びつけましょう。

Warming Up

CheckLink   DL 340 ~ 341   CD4-64 ~ CD4-65

音声を聞いて空所の語句を書き取り、質問に対する最も適切な答えを選びましょう。

Today, I'm happy to ¹_____ our Salesperson of the Year. This year, the ²_____ goes to Jake Miller. This was only Jake's ³_____ year with the ⁴_____, and he sold 155 ⁵_____. Well ⁶_____!

1. What is the purpose of this talk?
(A) To announce a sale
(B) To make an announcement
(C) To introduce a new product
(D) To thank a project team

141

2. How long has Jake worked for the company?

   (A) One year   (B) Two years   (C) Three years   (D) Four years

3. What does Jake sell?

   (A) Boats   (B) Houses   (C) Cars   (D) Paintings

 Now You Try!

CheckLink   DL 342 ~ 345   CD4-66 ~ CD4-69

会話を聞いて、質問に対する最も適切な答えを選びましょう。

Talk 1

1. What is the speaker discussing?

   (A) A training schedule

   (B) A sales report

   (C) New products

   (D) Results of a survey

2. What is the problem with their products?

   (A) Their prices are high.

   (B) They are not popular.

   (C) Their quality is not good.

   (D) They sold out in many regions.

3. What is the company's goal?

   (A) To have more sales

   (B) To offer more products

   (C) To reduce prices

   (D) To open more stores

Talk 2

Region	Sales
North America	2,000,000
South America	900,000
Europe	1,800,000
Asia	600,000

4. What does the speaker's company sell?

   (A) Computers

   (B) Digital cameras

   (C) Game software

   (D) Smartphones

5. Look at the graphic. Which region is the company worried about?

   (A) North America

   (B) South America

   (C) Europe

   (D) Asia

6. What is the company planning to do?

   (A) Hire more sales staff

   (B) Open more shops

   (C) Stop selling in Asia

   (D) Change its advertising plan

Vocabulary Builder Ⓑ

CheckLink 　DL 346 　CD4-70

次の 1 〜 8 の意味に合うものを a 〜 h から選びましょう。その後で、音声を聞いて答えを確認しましょう。

1. chart （　） **2.** decrease （　） **3.** successful （　） **4.** achieve （　）
5. goal （　） **6.** location （　） **7.** campaign （　） **8.** positive （　）

a. 目標　　　　　　 b. 達成する　　　　 c. 成功した　　　 d. キャンペーン
e. 場所、店舗　　　 f. 前向きな、積極的な　 g. 減少（する）　 h. 図、表、グラフ

Part 5 Sentence Completion 【短文穴埋め問題】

関係詞は複雑に思えるかもしれませんが、種類と使い方を覚えればそれほど難しくはありません。

関係詞の使い方

● 関係詞はすでに述べられた人や物に情報を追加します。同じ情報を繰り返さずに節と節をつなげる場合に使います。

I read a <u>book</u>. **It** *was interesting.* → *The <u>book</u>* **that** *I read was interesting.*

関係詞の種類

	情報を追加するもの	
who	人	*She's the woman* **who** *owns the jewelry company.* （彼女は宝石会社を所有している女性です）
that	物・人	*The train* **that** *I use is crowded.* （私が使う電車は混んでいます） *He's the man* **that** *I met at the party.* （彼は私がパーティーで会った男性です）
which	物	*The bag* **which** *I saw is cheap.* （私が見たバッグは安いです）
whose	人・物	*That's the woman* **whose** *wallet I found.* （あれは私が財布を見つけた女性です） *The house* **whose** *door is red is for sale.* （ドアが赤い家は売り出し中です）
when	時	*That was the year* **when** *we bought our house.* （あれは私たちが家を買った年でした）
where	場所	*This is the park* **where** *I usually eat lunch.* （ここは私がよくランチを食べる公園です）
why	理由	*He didn't tell me the reason* **why** *he quit.* （彼は辞めた理由を私に話しませんでした）

Warming Up

CheckLink

正しい選択肢を選び、文を完成させましょう。

1. He's the man (**a.** who   **b.** which) I met last week.
2. That's the writer (**a.** that   **b.** whose) book I am reading.
3. Rugby is a sport (**a.** that   **b.** when) is not very popular now.
4. The city (**a.** where   **b.** when) we live has many museums.

Now You Try!

CheckLink

4つの選択肢から最も適切なものを選び、文を完成させましょう。

1. Shoppers ------- buy the new product will receive a coupon.
   (A) who   (B) which   (C) where   (D) when

2. Please look at the chart ------- shows last year's sales.
   (A) who   (B) that   (C) whose   (D) when

3. July and August are months ------- many people buy air conditioners.
   (A) where   (B) which   (C) whose   (D) when

4. This is the only store ------- our sales have improved.
   (A) where   (B) who   (C) why   (D) when

5. No one knows the reason ------- we are losing customers.
   (A) whose   (B) why   (C) when   (D) where

6. The new smartphones ------- the company sells are popular.
   (A) when   (B) where   (C) who   (D) which

7. Bob Wilkins is a person ------- sales experience we need.
   (A) that   (B) who   (C) whose   (D) why

8. Our customers ------- shop online are between 20 and 40 years old.
   (A) which   (B) when   (C) who   (D) where

Part 6 Text Completion 【長文穴埋め問題】

空所に入る正しい文を選ぶ前に、まず全体を読むようにしましょう。何についての文章かを知ることで、正しい文を選びやすくなります。

Warming Up

 CheckLink

正しい選択肢を選び、文を完成させましょう。

1. (**a.** We will stop selling some of our products. **b.** We received the results of our customer survey.) They are very positive.

2. We need to change our marketing strategy. (**a.** Otherwise, our sales will continue to decrease. **b.** However, it was not very good.)

3. Please look at this sales report. (**a.** Sales are down in all of our stores. **b.** Sales are up 7%.) I think it is because our marketing campaign was very successful.

Now You Try!

 CheckLink

4 つの選択肢から最も適切なものを選び、文を完成させましょう。

Questions 1–4 refer to the following letter.

> Dear Mr. Collins,
>
> My name is Elaine Kelsey. I am the marketing ------- for Wellington Fitness
>   **1.**
> Equipment. Are you interested in introducing ------- products on your fitness blog?
>   **2.**
> -------. I would like to call or visit you this week and discuss the idea. I hope -------
> **3.**   **4.**
> from you soon.
>
> Kindest regards,
>
> Elaine Kelsey
> Wellington Fitness Equipment

1. (A) manager   (B) managing   (C) manages   (D) management

2. (A) we   (B) our   (C) us   (D) ours

3. (A) I exercise every day.   (B) We have two factories.
   (C) Technology is changing very quickly.   (D) Your followers will like them.

4. (A) hear   (B) hearing   (C) to hear   (D) heard

Part 7　Reading Comprehension　【読解問題】

複数の文書に関する問題では、質問に答えるためにすべての文書の情報が必要になることがあります。それぞれの文書の関連する情報を照らし合わせましょう。

Warming Up　　　　　　　　　　　　　C CheckLink

次の2つの文書を読んで質問に答えましょう。

Time	Subject	Presenter
1:00 P.M.	Sales	Brian Hawkins
1:30 P.M.	Survey	Lisa Ward
2:00 P.M.	Planning	George Dorsey
2:30 P.M.	New Products	Emily Carlson

William,

I would like to switch the 2:00 P.M. and 2:30 P.M. presentations. Please make the change before you send it to the sales and marketing team.

Holly Watson, Sales and Marketing Manager

What will be the subject of the 2:00 P.M. presentation after the change?

(A) Sales　　　(B) Survey　　　(C) Planning　　　(D) New products

Now You Try!　　　　　　　　　　　　C CheckLink

文書を読んで、設問に対する最も適切な答えを選びましょう。

Questions 1-5 refer to the following report and e-mail.

Date:	September 7
Title:	Marketing Campaign Report
Prepared by:	Terry Crawford, Assistant Marketing Manager

Store location	Manager	Number of customers JULY	Number of customers AUGUST	Increase in customers
Broad Street	Ron Wood	6,000	7,500	+25%
Maple Avenue	Mary Brown	5,000	5,900	+18%
Center Street	Mike Lind	4,000	4,400	+10%
Grand Avenue	Susan Hines	3,000	3,450	+15%

From:	Grace Kerns
To:	Terry Crawford
Date:	September 8
Subject:	Report

Dear Terry,

Thank you for your report on our August marketing campaign. Our campaign goal was a twenty percent increase in customers. One store achieved the goal, but the other three locations did not. I will visit all of the managers next week and discuss the campaign. I will start with the Center Street store on Monday.

Grace
Marketing Manager

1. What is the report mainly about?

   (A) A sale   (B) Results of a campaign

   (C) A marketing meeting   (D) A store opening

2. When was the campaign held?

   (A) In June   (B) In July   (C) In August   (D) In September

3. What was the goal of the campaign?

   (A) 10% more customers   (B) 15% more sales

   (C) 20% more customers   (D) 25% more sales

4. Which store location achieved the goal?

   (A) Broad Street   (B) Maple Avenue

   (C) Center Street   (D) Grand Avenue

5. Who will Ms. Kerns visit on Monday?

   (A) Ron Wood   (B) Mary Brown

   (C) Mike Lind   (D) Susan Hines

Vocabulary Builder Ⓐ & Ⓑ
各UnitのVocabulary Builderで取り上げた語句です

Unit 1　Shopping

coupon	名 割引券
customer	名 客
discount	名 割引　動 割引く
equipment	名 機器、用品
feedback	名 意見、反応
item	名 品物、商品
on sale	セール中で
order	名 注文　動 注文する
payment	名 支払い
product	名 製品
receipt	名 領収書、レシート
save	動 節約する
selection	名 選択、選ばれたもの
shop	名 店　動 買い物をする
shopper	名 買い物客
tool	名 道具

Unit 2　Dining Out

available	形 空いている、手に入る
chef	名 シェフ、料理人
confirm	動 確認する
crowded	形 混雑している
dessert	名 デザート
dish	名 皿、料理
excellent	形 素晴らしい
meal	名 食事
offer	名 申し出　動 申し出る
own	動 所有する
prepare	動 準備する
ready	形 準備ができた
reasonable	形 手ごろな
reservation	名 予約
serve	動 料理を出す
suggest	動 提案する

Unit 3　Daily Life

appointment	名 予約、約束
bill	名 請求書
clinic	名 診療所
clothes	名 洋服
electricity	名 電気
exercise	名 運動　動 運動する
follow	動 従う
join	動 加わる、参加する
library	名 図書館
medicine	名 薬
membership	名 会員（資格）
pharmacy	名 薬局
public	形 公共の、公の
reduce	動 減らす
renew	動 更新する
trash	名 ゴミ

Unit 4　Travel

airline	名 航空会社
arrival	名 到着
arrive	動 到着する
book	動 予約する
delay	名 遅延　動 遅らせる
depart	動 出発する
departure	名 出発
due to	…が原因で
fill out	記入する
flight	名 （飛行機の）便
luggage	名 手荷物
passenger	名 乗客
rate	名 料金
sightseeing	名 観光
tourist	名 観光客
travel agent	名 旅行業者

Unit 5 Entertainment

admission fee	名	入場料
amusement park	名	遊園地
art gallery	名	画廊
artwork	名	芸術作品
culture	名	文化
draw	動	描く
exhibit	名 展示 動	展示する
famous	形	有名な
museum	名	美術館、博物館
orchestra	名	オーケストラ
painting	名	絵画
perform	動	演奏する
performance	名	公演、演奏
review	名 評論 動	検討する
stadium	名	スタジアム、競技場
theater	名	劇場

Unit 6 News & Media

announce	動	発表する
article	名	記事
cause	名 原因 動	引き起こす
heavy snow	名	大雪
host	名 司会者 動	主催する
invite	動	招待する
local	形	地元の
photographer	名	写真家、カメラマン
press conference	名	記者会見
raise	動	上げる
report	名 報道 動	報道する
reporter	名	記者
temperature	名	気温
traffic	名	交通
volunteer	名 ボランティア 動	志願する
weather	名	天気

Unit 7 Housing

convenient	形	便利な
cost	名 費用 動	費用がかかる
design	名 設計 動	設計する
dormitory	名	寮
estimate	名 見積もり 動	見積もる
floor plan	名	間取り図
furniture	名	家具
garage	名	車庫、ガレージ
moving company	名	引っ越し会社
neighborhood	名	近所
plant	名 植物 動	植える
provide	動	提供する
real estate agent	名	不動産業者
rent	名 家賃 動	賃貸する
replace	動	取り替える
view	名	眺め

Unit 8 Office 1

assistance	名	支援、援助
cabinet	名	戸棚、キャビネット
cooperation	名	協力
co-worker	名	同僚
department	名	部、部門
device	名	機器、装置
document	名	書類
drawer	名	引き出し
maintenance	名	保守点検
office hours	名	業務時間
require	動	必要とする
set up		設定する
shelf	名	棚
stairs	名	階段
supply	名 備品 動	供給する
turn on		（電気などを）つける

Unit 9 Employment

accept	動	受け入れる
apply	動	応募する
candidate	名	候補者
degree	名	学位
employee	名	従業員
experience	名	経験
hire	動	雇う
interview	名	面接 動 面接する
introduce	動	紹介する
knowledge	名	知識
opening	名	職の空き
overtime	名 残業 形 時間外の 副 時間外に
paid vacation	名	有給休暇
position	名	職、立場
résumé	名	履歴書
retire	動	退職する

Unit 10 Meetings

absent	形	欠席して
agree	動	賛成する
attend	動	参加する、出席する
behind	副 遅れて 前 後ろに
business trip	名	出張
correct	動 訂正する 形 正しい
discuss	動	話し合う
explain	動	説明する
improve	動	改善する
meeting	名	会議、打ち合わせ
on schedule		予定通りに
policy	名	方針
postpone	動	延期する
project	名	計画
propose	動	提案する
reschedule	動	予定を変更する

Unit 11 Clients

apologize	動	謝罪する
client	名	顧客
contact	名 連絡 動 連絡する
continue	動	続く、続ける
contract	名	契約（書）
deliver	動	配達する
fill in		記入する
in cash		現金で
increase	名 増加 動 増加する
missing	形	見つからない
negotiate	動	交渉する
order form	名	注文用紙、注文書
promote	動	促進する、宣伝する
relationship	名	関係
safety	名	安全
sign	動	署名する

Unit 12 Office 2

away	形	離れて
branch	名	支店、支社
complete	動 完成する 形 完全な
deadline	名	締め切り、期限
enter	動	入る
guard	名	守衛、警備員
ID card	名	身分証明書
install	動	設置する
laptop	名	ノートパソコン
management	名	経営（陣）
motivation	名	やる気、動機
on business		仕事で
on time		時間通りに
proposal	名	提案
security	名	安全
submit	動	提出する

Unit 13 Computers & Technology

allow	動	許す
app	名	アプリケーション
automatic	形	自動の
collaboration	名	協力、共同作業
develop	動	発展させる
engineer	名	技術者
factory	名	工場
mobile	形	携帯電話の、モバイルの
monitor	名	モニター 動 監視する
operate	動	操作する、作動する
production	名	生産
protect	動	保護する
strength	名	強み
turn off	名	（電気などを）消す
update	名	更新 動 更新する
virtual	形	仮想の、事実上の

Unit 14 Events

annual	形	毎年恒例の
celebration	名	お祝い、祝賀会
charity	名	慈善
city hall	名	市役所
conference	名	（大きな）会議
festival	名	祭
guest	名	ゲスト、招待客
hold	動	開催する
invitation	名	招待（状）
opening ceremony	名	開会式、開幕式
reception	名	歓迎会、受付
register for		登録する
seminar	名	セミナー
take place		行われる
useful	形	役に立つ
workshop	名	研修会

Unit 15 Sales & Marketing

achieve	動	達成する
advertising	名	宣伝（活動）
award	名	賞 動 賞を与える
best-selling	形	最も売れている
budget	名	予算
campaign	名	キャンペーン
chart	名	図、表、グラフ
decrease	名	減少 動 減少する
goal	名	目標
location	名	場所、店舗
positive	形	前向きな、積極的な
region	名	地域
sales report	名	営業報告書
strategy	名	戦略
successful	形	成功した
survey	名	調査 動 調査する

本書には CD（別売）があります

FIRST TRY
FOR THE TOEIC® L&R TEST

基本文法 & 語彙ではじめる TOEIC® L&R テスト

2023 年 1 月 20 日　初版第 1 刷発行
2024 年 2 月 20 日　初版第 4 刷発行

著　者　Robert Hickling

発行者　福　岡　正　人

発行所　株式会社　金星堂

（〒 101-0051）東京都千代田区神田神保町 3-21
Tel. (03) 3263-3828（営業部）
(03) 3263-3997（編集部）
Fax (03) 3263-0716
https://www.kinsei-do.co.jp

編集担当　今門貴浩　　　　　　　　　　　　Printed in Japan
印刷所・製本所／大日本印刷株式会社

ISBN978-4-7647-4182-9　C1082